W9-BKA-303

EXTRAORDINARY AMERICAN INDIANS

EXTRAORDINARY AMERICAN INDIANS

By Susan Avery and Linda Skinner

Consultants

Jay Miller, Ph.D.
Newberry Library

Pat Locke
MacArthur Foundation Fellow

Helen Chalakee Burgess
Deputy Director
Oklahoma Indian Affairs Commission

CHILDRENS PRESS ®
CHICAGO

The authors wish to acknowledge substantial contributions to the researching and writing of a number of the articles in this book. Thanks are due to Charnan Simon for the biographies of Frederick Dockstader, Donald Pelotte, Buffy Sainte-Marie, and Will Sampson. Alice Flanagan gave the essay on the Iroquois Confederacy its present form and direction. Interviews and inquiries by Ann Duvall provided useful information on several contemporary figures.

Two articles draw heavily on single sources. The biography of Clarence Tinker is based mainly on "Osage Aviator: The Life and Career of Major General Clarence L. Tinker," by James L. Crowder, Jr., Chronicles of Oklahoma 65 (Winter 1987 1988): 400–431. The biography of Frank Fools Crow leans on Thomas E. Mails' book *Fools Crow* (Doubleday, 1985).

Picture acknowledgments appear on pages 249 and 250.

Grateful acknowledgment is made for permission to reprint the following copyrighted material: "It Doesn't End, of Course," by Simon Ortiz, from *Going for the Rain*, ©1976 by Simon Ortiz. Reprinted by permission of Harper & Row, New York.
"Remember," by Joy Harjo, from *She Had Some Horses*, ©1983 Thunder's Mouth Press. Reprinted by permission of the publisher.

Project Editors:
    E. Russell Primm III and Alice Flanagan

Electronic Design and Page Composition:
    Lindaanne Donohoe

Photo Researcher: Carol Parden

Senior Editor: Charnan Simon

Copyeditors: Charnan Simon, Nancy McKearn

Editorial Assistant: Mark Friedman

Researcher: Ann Duvall

Library of Congress
Cataloging-in-Publication Data

Avery, Susan
Extraordinary American Indians / Susan Avery and Linda Skinner
    p. cm.
Summary: Discusses the lives and accomplishments of outstanding Native Americans from the eighteenth century to the present, including Wilma Mankiller, Billy Mills, Sacagawea, Louis Ballard, and Will Rogers.
ISBN 0-516-00583-9
1. Indians of North America—Biography—Juvenile literature. [1. Indians of North America—Biography.] I. Title.

E89.A88 1992
973'0497—dc20   92-11358
CIP   AC

Copyright© 1992 Childrens Press®, Inc. All rights reserved.
Published simultaneously in Canada. Printed in the United States of America.
1 2 3 4 5 6 7 8 9 R 01 00 99 98 97 96 95 94 93

Contents

Introduction

Just as the yarns in the fine Navajo weaving on the cover of this book are interlaced, some running across each other, some running parallel, so human lives are woven together. Each life, like the yarns of the textile, takes an individual path that is slightly different from any other, and one person's life can directly touch relatively few others. Yet each separate and independent strand in a beautiful fabric has its place, contributing a necessary part to an intricate pattern that emerges for the viewer who steps back and surveys the whole. Similarly, the stories of individual lives, woven together, can suggest a picture of a diverse people, their varied cultural traditions, and their enduring presence on a continent.

The authors of *Extraordinary American Indians* hope that the individuals and events described in this book will help form such a richly patterned picture for its readers. The brief accounts presented here highlight the activities and contributions of several dozen outstanding Indian men and women. They are people from various regions of North America, from different native nations, different eras, and different walks of life. The lives and achievements of each person illustrate some notable aspect of the American Indian experience, past and present. Taken together, their stories may give readers a deeper sense of the heritage shared by all Americans, both Indian and non-Indian.

No book like this can possibly reflect the full range and richness of the American Indian world. There are today hundreds of Indian nations, languages, and cultures flourishing within the borders of the United States. Their diversity and sheer numbers have meant that they could not all be represented. Nor has any attempt been made to outline the whole history of the peoples native to this continent.

Instead, the authors have presented the stories of one selection of truly exceptional Indian people. Some of their names will be familiar; others may not be so. All of these people have made significant contributions to their own nation's welfare as well as to the broader human community. There are many, many other individuals whose stories could also have been told, because their accomplishments, their courage and determination, their spiritual wisdom, or other qualities are likewise remarkable.

So think of these short biographies and essays as lending texture and complexity to a much larger picture. Glimpse in these small stories the ordeal of all Indian peoples, and the survival and continuing vitality of Indian cultures. The authors hope that as the stories weave together, readers will be led to explore more of the vast panorama, and also that the examples of extraordinary individuals included here can reveal new possibilities for achievement in the readers' own lives.

Susan Avery
August 1992

෯ ෯ ෯ ෯

Foreword

Long before Christopher Columbus and his band of sailors landed on the Caribbean Islands in 1492, thinking they had reached India, native peoples in the Americas had developed diverse cultures—some even rivaling advanced civilizations elsewhere. Although some lived in small, simple communities and survived by hunting and gathering food, other village cultures successfully learned how to cultivate corn and beans and gradually flourished into city states and powerful empires.

Between A.D. 250 and 900 the Mayan people in southern Mexico and Central America had developed one of the highest civilizations known in the early world. It is generally believed that their country extended over an area as large as modern Italy. From remains and historical accounts, we know that their leaders had built great temple-pyramids, a system of bridges and aqueducts, and astronomical observatories. They had created a system of writing using hieroglyphs, a number system, lunar and solar calendars, and made incredible advances in agriculture, art, and science. From their monuments we have learned a great deal about their personal lives and important families.

But the Mayans were not alone in the quickly expanding world of their time. In Mexico, the Olmecs (1200 B.C. to A.D. 600), the Toltec empire (A.D. 900 to A.D. 1200), and the Aztec empire (A.D. 1325 to 1521) all had made significant advances. The Aztecs, however, were by far the largest and busiest trading center of all.

In North America there is evidence that people in the Ohio Valley were making pottery and building burial mounds several centuries before the beginning of the Maya Classic Age. As early as A.D. 1, people were planting corn in the region we call Arizona. The practice spread throughout the region to the Basketmakers of the Southwest—ancestors of the modern Pueblo Indians. Here, where New Mexico, Arizona, Utah, and Colorado join, the Golden Age of the Pueblos flourished. In time, trade routes spiraled out from these areas, connecting to each other and to markets as far away as Mexico and Central America. Pottery, spun-cotton materials, feathers, animal skins, salt, rubber, yarn, rope, carved jade and turquoise items, sea-shells, copper, paints, and dyes were among the many things that exchanged hands along land and water routes. More importantly, ideas were exchanged and religious, political, and social customs were shared.

It is believed that a trade route by sea reached across the Gulf of Mexico to the Mississippi River where a great alliance of prosperous nations existed. Between A.D. 700 and 1600, Mississippians had built a network of trade with people from the Great Lakes to the Gulf of Mexico and from the Atlantic Ocean to what is now Oklahoma.

The world has been fed in mind and body by these early Native Americans who left us systems for writing, counting, and telling time. Skilled farmers not only introduced corn, potatoes, peppers, tomatoes, beans, squash, cacao, cotton, rubber, and tobacco to the world but also devised ways of irrigating and preserving crops that are still used today. Astronomers and farmers left us techniques for knowing when and how to plant and harvest crops and how to understand the skies.

Master builders left monuments of their skill and artistry. Among the most impressive in the United States are the clustered stone-walled towns in Chaco Canyon, New Mexico, which flourished from A.D. 800 to 1100, and the earthen mound and temple complex at Cahokia near St. Louis, Missouri, which was the largest town on the Mississippi River by A.D. 1200.

From native healers and spiritual leaders came medicines and methods for curing illnesses that are an essential part of the medical field today. Among the most honored Indian leaders in North America were healers, prophets, and priests who conducted ceremonies to cure illness and prepare for or give thanks for special events. The source of some of these religious traditions were special messengers or intermediaries such as White Buffalo Calf Woman of the Lakota, and Sweet Medicine of the Cheyenne.

Our ways of viewing the world and responding to it have been influenced by the religious and philosophical beliefs of native cultures and oral traditions, which carry knowledge, history, and information about cultural heroes to other generations. Native American cultural heroes often had animal names, such as coyote, raven, buffalo, and rabbit, and were gifted with all the attributes of human beings. For many native people of North America, certain animals also possessed powers to create such things as rivers and mountains, customs and taboos.

Today, mainstream Americans honor most of the same kinds of people that have always been respected by native peoples. Athletes, artists, scientists, military heros, doctors, and spiritual leaders have always had their place of honor, but in Indian society, these roles were filled by both men and women.

Indeed, before there was an America by name, its native people were making extraordinary contributions to its growth and development. Today there are more than 500 Indian nations in the United States with governing documents recognized by the federal government. American Indian citizens in these communities are playing significant roles in business, medicine, education, government, and the arts. By acknowledging their contributions and the living legacy of past generations of native cultures, we can put our modern world in perspective. Only then will we begin to understand the extent to which these contributions have affected the direction of the United States and the future of the planet earth.

ยา ยา ยา ยา

Note to the Reader

Whenever the birth and death dates for a person are known they have been included. Sometimes the dates are less than certain or are completely unknown. Those dates followed with a question mark indicate a lack of certainty about the probable date cited. A lesser degree of certainty is indicated by the abbreviation *c.* (for the Latin word circa meaning about or approximately) before the date. A question mark with no date attached at all indicates absolute uncertainty.

The names of some American Indian peoples have several spellings in the English language. Where one is preferred (such as Odawa, for example) that name is given first with the alternative spelling given in parentheses (Ottawa).

&a &a &a &a

A Note on the Art

The colorful textile on the cover of *Extraordinary American Indians* is a blanket woven by the Navajo and is now in the collections of the Museum of New Mexico. The American Indians pictured on the cover are as follows (from left to right):

First Row: Ishi, Sequoyah

Second Row: La Donna Harris

Third Row: Sitting Bull, Charles Curtis, Jim Thorpe

Fourth Row: Will Rogers

Fifth Row: Maria Martinez, Maria Tallchief

Sixth Row: Clarence Tinker, Tecumseh

The intricate borders that appear on each page of the book were drawn by Lindaanne Donohoe, the book's designer. The elements depicted in the borders are from tribes from different regions of the country.

Southwest→

Southwest ↘

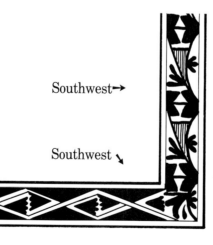

Pope
San Juan Pueblo resistance leader
?–1692?

He believed he was led by his ancestor spirits, the *oxua*, who were angry at how the Pueblo Indians had abandoned their traditional religion and customs. Pope clung defiantly to the old Pueblo ways, despite more than eighty years of domination of his people by Spanish civil and religious authorities. With great cunning and determination, Pope secretly organized a revolt that threw out the Spanish conquerors, at least for a dozen years. More than three centuries later, Pope is remembered as the native leader who was most successful in organizing native peoples to drive European invaders from the West.

There are no records of Pope before 1675 when he first came into conflict with the Spanish colonial government. He was then an obscure, middle-aged Tewa medicine man of San Juan Pueblo, which was one of many pueblos, or villages, in what is now part of New Mexico and Arizona. For generations, Spanish landlords had forced the pueblo-dwellers to work as serfs on large estates called *encomiendas*, while Spanish priests had insisted that the Pueblo people give up their own religious beliefs and practice Catholicism. Life continued in this uneasy peace for more than eighty years. Then, in the latter half of the 1600s, drought, famine, disease, and increasing clashes with their Apache neighbors made life worse for the Pueblo people. Pope was one of many Pueblo holy men who began to resist Spanish authority and to preach a return to the old ways.

In 1675, Spanish officials rounded up forty-seven rebellious leaders, including Pope. Three were hanged, the rest were flogged and imprisoned. Only after a delegation of angry Indians demanded their release did the Spaniards let the prisoners go.

The experience hardened Pope's already militant resolve to drive out the oppressors. Hiding out at Taos Pueblo, he carefully plotted a large-scale uprising. He met secretly with trusted leaders from other pueblos and sent messages across the region to Indians still farther away. Pope was shrewd and merciless with possible traitors; he even had his own son-in-law killed when he suspected him of betraying the rebellion. By the summer of 1680, Pope was ready. Runners went out to leaders of the Tewa, Tiwa, and Keres peoples in the pueblos along the Rio Grande, to the Zuni and Hopi to the west, and even to the Apaches. The runners carried knotted cords as coded messages, setting August 11 as the date for the revolt. To those leaders he suspected of being informers, Pope sent other cords to trick them into believing the attack would take place on August 13.

For the Pueblo, running was both a sport and a means of communication.

The Spaniards were surprised and stunned by the sudden massive attack. The Indians first struck outlying settlements of Spanish colonists. Soon after that, a force of about 500 warriors besieged the Spanish capital at Santa Fe. The fighting was fierce. Within days, some four hundred colonists were dead, including twenty-one of thirty-three missionary priests. Nearly all of the remaining 2,400 settlers had fled south toward El Paso, leaving the Pueblo people in firm control of their own lands.

Now Pope and his followers set about destroying almost all traces of the Spanish occupation of the region, from household goods to churches to government records. They severely punished anyone who appeared reluctant to give up the Spanish language, Spanish names, and especially Roman Catholic ceremonies. Pope himself traveled from pueblo to pueblo, overseeing the destruction of everything Spanish and the restoration of the traditional Pueblo Indian life.

After a period of rejoicing at their liberation, the Pueblo people began to realize how hard it was to resume a way of life they had not known for decades. They missed the tools and other practical items that the Spaniards had introduced. Then, too, they had been governed by the Spaniards for so long that the traditional Pueblo system of law and order seemed unfamiliar. They had also grown used to the powerful support of Spanish soldiers and their European armaments. Without the additional defense of Spanish soldiers, the Pueblo people came under increasing attack by roving bands of raiders from other tribes.

Faced with growing unrest within the pueblos and uncertainty from without, Pope ruled more and more like a tyrannical Spanish governor. He demanded that people bow in his presence; he ordered harsh punishments or execution for his opponents; he used prisoners as slaves; he even rode around Santa Fe in the old Spanish governor's carriage. Faced with such treatment, several Pueblo groups retaliated, driving Pope from power. By 1688, however, Pope reestablished his rule.

In 1692 the Spanish army reclaimed Santa Fe, a new Spanish governor took over, and the reconquest of New Mexico became official.

Pope was gone and the revolt he led was over, yet the rebellion spurred lasting changes. Spanish colonial authorities changed their administrative policies, reducing the power of the Catholic Church and eliminating the *encomienda* system.

But another change was more far-reaching. When the Spaniards retreated south in 1680, they left behind horses. The descendants of those Spanish horses spread far and wide, transforming the lifestyles of many native peoples. By the middle of the 1700s, Plains Indians had made horses an essential part of their culture. The mounted warriors and buffalo hunters of the Plains, who proved to be such skilled opponents of white soldiers and settlers, thus owed their success, at least in part, to the Pueblo leader Pope.

ଈ ଈ ଈ ଈ

Pontiac
Odawa military and political leader
*c.*1720–1769

Nothing is certain about his early life, and mystery surrounds his death. What is clear is that Pontiac, a chief of the Odawa (Ottawa) nation, organized and led one of the greatest military alliances in American Indian history. He was trying to pre-serve Indian independence from European powers, but his success proved short-lived and dissolved in a matter of months. Traditional stories tell only that Pontiac was probably born in an Odawa village in Ohio around 1720, and that one of his parents was Odawa and the other was Ojibwa (Chippewa). During his childhood, the French dominated the region from the Ohio River Valley north to the Great Lakes. Most Indians in the area were allies of the French and supported them in a series of wars against the British. Pontiac himself may have fought in one such war in 1746. He almost certainly fought in the French and Indian War, starting in 1754. In 1760, France, until then the major European power in Canada, surrendered most of it to Britain, thus effectively ending the war. But the British and French did not formally make peace right away.

For the French-allied natives in the region, the unfortunate aspect of this surrender was that British troops and agents took over the French forts and trading posts. Many of the French had been rather easygoing in their dealings with the Indians. With the coming of the British, however, Indians were no longer welcome at the forts, and trade goods that the French had exchanged for furs came to an end. Moreover, the British, unlike the French, would not sell or trade many items that the Indians had come to rely on, and they did not hesitate to take over Indian ancestral lands.

By 1755, Pontiac was chief of a loose confederacy of Odawa, Potawatomi, and Ojibwa tribes. In 1762, he heard the message of Neolin, a spiritual leader known as the Delaware Prophet. The Prophet preached that Indians should turn aside all white influences and return to their traditional ways. Doing so, the Prophet said, would soon cause all the white people to be driven away. Pontiac began preaching a similar message, but he emphasized driving away British people.

Pontiac was an inspiring speaker with great oratorical skills. As Indian discontent with the British grew, so did the number of Pontiac's followers. By early 1763, he had the support of practically every Indian tribe in the region. Pontiac told them that if they worked together, they could drive the British out, and that in this effort they would have the help of their old allies, the French. His plan was for each tribe to attack the nearest fort and then destroy undefended British frontier settlements.

Pontiac wanted his own warriors to launch a surprise attack on the British at Fort Detroit. But two attempts to attack failed. So in May 1763, Pontiac began a siege of Detroit and gave the signal for the other tribes to attack the other forts. The siege at Detroit dragged on for months. Elsewhere in the region other parts of the alliance had better success. In less than two months, tribes of the alliance captured or forced the abandonment of nine major forts, leaving only three in British hands, with two of those, including Detroit, under siege.

The Indians also won battles in areas away from the forts. In May, Pontiac's warriors beat back British units trying to resupply Detroit. Two months later, they defeated a large party of soldiers who had emerged from Detroit in an effort to break the siege. Throughout the region, Indians, in an effort to stop whites moving into their territory, attacked frontier settlements, killing hundreds of settlers and sending thousands more retreating eastward across the Appalachian Mountains.

Despite these victories, by summer's end the campaign was stalling. The military blockade of the forts was not succeeding. Indian fighters were not accustomed to siege warfare, and even Pontiac's great leadership skills could not keep them from losing interest. As winter approached, the warriors became worried about providing food for their families, and more and more abandoned the siege to go home. Supply boats got through to Detroit, and fresh British troops began arriving in the region. One by one, the tribes in Pontiac's alliance began to withdraw.

Pontiac's great oratory skill enhanced his ability to lead his people.

The final blow came in October. Word arrived that the British and French had finally made peace, and despite what Pontiac had been led to believe, there would be no French military assistance. By the middle of November, Pontiac's campaign was over. He did not give up, however. For the next year and a half, Pontiac traveled around the region trying to rouse the tribes for a new campaign. Many Indians were ready to fight but only if they were attacked, and the British were careful not to do that.

By early 1765, Pontiac realized that all of his allies were gone, and he consented to meet with the British military command. At the meeting, Pontiac agreed that all fighting would end and that Indians and British would live in peace. After signing a treaty in 1766, Pontiac kept his word and never renewed his campaign.

Although Pontiac's alliance ended in failure, it may have stimulated beneficial changes. The British government issued the Royal Proclamation of 1763, prohibiting white settlements west of the Allegheny Mountains. Many whites violated the Proclamation, but it temporarily slowed the advance of settlers. Also, reforms intended to improve trade practices with the Indians were put in place. They formed the basis of British policy that partially protected Indian interests. Ultimately, the British did not honor the terms of the 1766 treaty and the Proclamation of 1763 had little long-term effect.

Perhaps Pontiac's willingness to make and then to keep the peace with the British had the greatest long-term significance for native peoples. He was an honorable man and a patriot. Future Indian patriots, such as Tecumseh, would continue in Pontiac's tradition of leadership and honor.

෩ ෩ ෩ ෩

Nancy Ward

Cherokee leader and peace advocate

c.1738–1822?

Although some Cherokees believed Nancy Ward betrayed her people, many listened with interest to what she had to say. Part of the reason may have been her commanding manner, but she also impressed people with the good sense of what she said. She tried to promote cooperation between whites and her own people, the Cherokees, during an era of mistrust and sometimes open warfare between the two groups. In the end, her views were swept aside, and the Cherokee people lost control of their ancestral homelands in the southern Appalachians. Yet Nancy Ward became the subject of many stories, and she is still remembered with affection by many throughout the region.

Her Cherokee name was Nanye'hi, but settlers later called her Nancy because that name sounded more familiar to them. She was born in the mountain forests of eastern Tennessee, probably in the Cherokee town of Chota, by the Little Tennessee River. Her family included several major Cherokee leaders. Nancy was married when she was quite young to a man named Kingfisher, with whom she had two children.

In Cherokee society, women traditionally have considerable authority and importance, both within the family and in the councils of government. In the past a few women also took part in warfare. Nancy, acting within Cherokee tradition, became known for fighting in the battle of 1755 against the Cherokees' frequent enemies, the Muscogee (Creeks). When Kingfisher was killed in this battle, she leaped to take his place and helped her people to win.

For her valor in battle, Nancy was recognized as "Agi-ga-u-e," meaning "Beloved Woman." By Cherokee tradition, this title, which was granted for life, meant that she was the leader of the Women's Council, a member of the Council of Chiefs, and could, on her own, pardon condemned prisoners.

Several years later Nancy married an Irish-born trader, Bryant (or Brian) Ward. After the birth of a daughter, he returned to his former home in South Carolina.

About this same time, the Cherokees were beginning to lose their traditional lands and livelihood to settlers. Along with other Indian groups, the Cherokees were drawn into the destructive Seven Years War, a conflict among European powers about control of territory in North America. When that war ended in 1763, many Cherokee were homeless, sick, hungry, or dead, and the tribe was

This cherokee house of the early 1800s is similar to the one Nancy Ward lived in while she ran her inn.

forced to give up much of its land. With more land open, the previous trickle of settlers moving into Cherokee territory of the southern Appalachians soon became a flood.

When the American Revolution broke out, most Cherokees supported the British. Partly this was because the British seemed more likely than the American colonists to restrain the flood of settlers moving into Indian territory. But once again, Cherokee lands and towns were ravaged by a war in which they sided with the loser, and at the end they were forced to give up more of their lands.

Despite an atmosphere of hostility between Indians and Americans during these years, Nancy Ward tried to develop friendly contacts in the nearby settlements in eastern Tennessee. She seems to have felt that resisting the heavily armed whites was useless and that it was better to make friends with the invaders than to fight them.

In 1776, Nancy warned nearby settlers that some pro-British Cherokees were planning to attack them. Later, when the settlers attacked the Cherokee-held part of the region in return, they spared Nancy Ward's village of Chota, in recognition of her friendship. She also stepped in when a settler captured by the Cherokees, a Mrs. Bean, was about to be put to death. Using her right as Agi-ga-u-e, Nancy arranged for the woman to stay in the household of a family member.

An interesting consequence of this episode was that Nancy learned about dairy cattle and making butter and cheese from Mrs. Bean. After the war, Nancy bought some cattle and introduced dairy farming to the Cherokees, a move that helped strengthen their economy.

In 1780, Nancy again warned the settlers of a planned attack, this time urging them to try peace talks instead of a counterattack. This effort was unsuccessful, and the Cherokee were defeated in the battles that followed. Nonetheless, in later negotiations, it was Nancy Ward who spoke for the tribe, urging peaceful solutions to the problems between Indians and whites.

By 1817, toward the end of her life, Nancy had come to feel that too much land had been lost too easily, and she tried to persuade the other Cherokee leaders to hold onto what was left. By then, however, it was too late. The old processes for making decisions in the tribe were changing, and a new group of chiefs agreed to give up still more territory, including Nancy's home, Chota. Forced to move, she opened an inn for travelers near Benton, Tennessee, where she died a few years later.

After her death, many remembered that Nancy Ward had tried to build a bridge of friendship between Indians and whites. Fanciful legends grew up concerning her powers and her beauty, and some of these were woven into the writings of well-known nineteenth-century storytellers.

The Iroquois Confederacy

It may never be known when the Iroquois Confederacy was founded. Historians estimate that perhaps four or five hundred years ago, five feuding Indian nations living in what is now New York state formed an alliance. According to Iroquois tradition, the idea for a federal union came from Deganwidah, a Huron, and his spokesman Hiawatha, who negotiated with leaders of the warring nations. Eventually, peace was procured, a constitution—the Great Law of Peace—was recorded on wampum belts, and a confederacy of tribes was formed, united against their enemies.

The Iroquois peoples lived in long, narrow birchbark structures, called longhouses. They used the longhouse as a symbol for the Confederacy, because the lands of member nations extended across the region. In this symbol, the Mohawks were the Keepers of the Eastern Door, the Senecas were the Keepers of the Western Door, and in between from east to west were the Oneidas, Onondagas, and Cayugas. The Onondagas were Keepers of the Fire. Even today, the members of these tribes refer to themselves as Haudenosaunee, meaning People of the Longhouse.

The tribes that make up the Six Nations of the Iroquois Confederacy can be seen at the middle and upper right of this map.

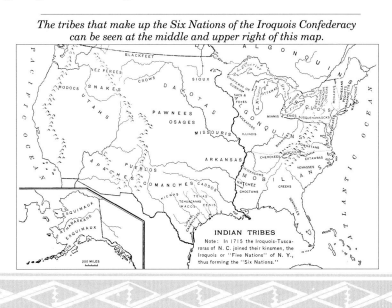

INDIAN TRIBES

Note: In 1715 the Iroquois-Tuscaroras of N. C. joined their kinsmen, the Iroquois or "Five Nations" of N. Y., thus forming the "Six Nations."

200 MILES

The text of the Great Law of Peace begins with the planting of the Tree of the Great Peace (a great white pine), which has four White Roots of Peace, extending in the four directions. Atop the tree is an eagle that screams a warning when danger comes near. The tree, which was located at the center of the confederacy, was on land of the Onondaga nation near the present site of Syracuse, New York.

The Great Law regarded Iroquois leaders as servants of the people and made provisions for their impeachment for improper behavior. It supported freedom of expression in political and religious matters; forbade unauthorized entry into homes; provided for political participation by women; mandated equal distribution of wealth; and provided for changes to the constitution by way of amendment.

Each member nation in the Confederacy took care of its own internal affairs, but in the Iroquois council, they shared joint international concerns about peace and war. Member tribes pledged that the Confederacy would act only if all could agree. They had to "be of one mind"; otherwise, the issues would be set aside and the council fire "covered with ashes." Fifty hereditary peace chiefs, or sachems, managed the civil affairs of the Confederacy. The presiding chief Atotarho (the name of the office) was appointed for life, but could be impeached for violating the Great Law of Peace.

The Confederacy served the Haudenosaunee well for a long time. Factions sometimes arose within it, but in general the Five Nations were prosperous and secure at home. In 1722, the Tuscaroras joined the Confederacy, and the Five Nations became the Six Nations. The Confederacy achieved its peak of strength and importance in the 1600s and 1700s, during a time when several European powers were attempting to become masters of North America. The Iroquois, skillful at pitting one European colonial power against the other, used the situation to their advantage. As the French and English fought over territory, the Iroquois increased their far-reaching connections to allied tribes and strengthened their control of the best trade route between the coast and the interior.

By 1754, to keep the French from settling the region, the American colonies had allied themselves with the Iroquois and other Indians along the northern frontier. In June 1754, a meeting of colonial commissioners and Iroquois sachems (called the Albany Congress) resulted in the Carlisle Treaty—an Anglo/Iroquois alliance against the French, and a colonial plan of union. Benjamin Franklin, who was well known among the Indians and an advocate of colonial union, was most influential at this congress. He presented a colonial plan of union that reflected England's demands for control of the colonies, the colonists desire for autonomy from England, and the Iroquois confederacy structure and philosophy.

Influenced by conversations with leaders of the Iroquois Confederacy and intrigued by the example of their constitution, the American colonies eventually formed a similar union in common defense under a common federal government. The Pennsylvania colony under the astute leadership of Benjamin Franklin played a key role in realizing the formation of the union and framing its constitution. Although both England and colonial leaders were not ready for Franklin's plan at this time and rejected it, later it would be repackaged by Franklin as the Articles of Confederation and then blended into the philosophical principles of the U.S. Constitution.

By 1763, England's war with the French in America had been won and the Iroquois Confederacy had been mortally weakened by feuds over whether the Confederacy should now support England or the colonies. The Oneidas and Tuscaroras felt that the rebelling colonists would eventually succeed in taking the land, and that therefore the Iroquois would be better off if they were allied with them. The rest of the Six Nations wanted to join with the British, because the British government seemed more likely to restrict the number of white settlers into Iroquois lands. Divisions within the confederacy, which led to fighting in the Grand Council at Onondaga, helped to destroy the confederacy's hold on the region. Thousands of new European immigrants, refusing to be bound by local treaty agreements, moved into Iroquois country and undermined peaceful relations between colonists and Indians. Several peaceful Indian settlements were attacked and hundreds killed. During the late 1770s, the thirteen American colonies, quickly approaching a federal union of states, became the most important confederacy in the region where once the Iroquois had been dominant.

When the Constitution of the United States was written in 1787, there were remarkable parallels to the "Great Law of Peace" of the Iroquois Confederacy, established perhaps before 1500. Scholars argue over how much and in what ways the Iroquois Confederacy influenced the U.S. Constitution, but interpretations of comments by framers of the government reveal that they not only knew about the Iroquois Confederacy, but found it an interesting example to consider.

In the Iroquois council, members from the Six Nations discussed matters of both war and peace.

Benjamin Franklin, who wrote the Albany Plan in 1754 that laid the groundwork for the U.S. Constitution, referred to the connection between the Iroquois Confederacy and a similar plan for colonial union in a letter to James Parker in 1751:

> It would be a very strange thing if Six Nations . . . should be capable of forming a Scheme for such an Union and be able to execute it in such a manner, as that it has subsisted Ages, and appears indissoluble, and yet a like Union should be impracticable for ten or a dozen English colonies.

Historians who have compared the Great Law of Peace and the U.S. Constitution cannot deny the obvious similarities of philosophy and political and social organization. Both documents propose local self-governments; a national confederation; elected leadership; popular suffrage; recall of leaders; legislative councils where every delegate has the right to vote and the right to be heard; referendum; initiative; and amendment. Both documents support the right of personal freedoms and promote general welfare over self-interest; mutual accomodation; balance and harmony; and the pursuit of happiness.

An inspiration for the framers of the U.S. Constitution and, perhaps, for a number of other social and political reform movements of the 1700s and 1800s, the remarkable Iroquois Confederacy is still provoking us to examine the relationship between a government and its people.

Joseph Brant
Mohawk chief, British soldier, and missionary
*c.*1742–1807

Joseph Brant lived in both the white world and the Indian world, and learned to survive in both. He was a Mohawk war captain whose very name struck terror in the hearts of white settlers living in regions that felt the force of his attacks. Yet he also adopted white ways and became a devout Christian missionary with the privileges of a British gentleman. He was a skilled diplomat and effective spokesman for his people, but during the American Revolution, he was instrumental in dividing the Iroquois Confederacy and bringing some of its leadership into a fateful alliance with the losing side.

Brant, whose Mohawk name was Thayendanegea ("two sticks of wood bound together"), was born about 1742 into a family that had already produced several distinguished leaders. His stepfather, Nichus Brant, was a Mohawk chief, and his grandfather had visited the court of Queen Anne in England. His older sister, Degonwadonti (Molly Brant), a very influential woman in her own right, was the wife of Sir William Johnson, the British superintendent of northern Indian affairs who was adopted by the Mohawk tribe and made their official representative to the Iroquois League.

Brant grew up in what is now central New York state. In his childhood, the farms and forts of colonists were already scattered across the region, which was the homeland of the Mohawk nation and the other nations that made up the Iroquois Confederacy. Brant grew up familiar with the traditional Iroquois

ways, but he was also friends with Sir Johnson's nephew, Guy Johnson, and with his son, John Johnson. By the age of thirteen, Brant was fighting in support of the British, first in the French and Indian War, and later in other military campaigns.

Sir William, impressed with the young Brant's intelligence, sent him to a school in Connecticut that was open to both white and Indian youths. Brant attended the school from the time he was nineteen until he was twenty-two. He learned to read and write English and the Mohawk language, and he studied European history and literature. He converted to Christianity and began his lifelong project of translating the Bible into Mohawk.

After Sir William died in 1774, Guy Johnson became the new superintendent, and he appointed Brant as his principal aide. The following year the Revolutionary War broke out. Brant allied himself with the British, partly

Sir William Johnson

because of his personal relationships, but also because of his conviction that the Iroquois would be better off if British rule continued. Along with many other Iroquois, he feared that an independent American nation would encourage more settlers to move into Iroquois territory.

Brant was commissioned a British army officer and went with Johnson to England to confer with government ministers. There he was received as the leader of the Mohawk nation, entertained by many important people, and treated as a celebrity.

A meeting of the Iroquois in front of Johnson Hall, the home of Sir William Johnson

In 1776, Brant returned home and began traveling from village to village, trying to rally his fellow Iroquois to take up arms against the Americans. In July 1777, four of the six Iroquois nations—the Mohawks, Onondagas, Cayugas, and Senecas—agreed to join with the British, with Brant as their war chief. But the other two nations of the Iroquois Confederacy—the Oneidas and Tuscaroras—sided with the Americans.

The once-powerful Confederacy was ruptured by dissension. Within weeks, the two Iroquois factions clashed at Oriskany in one of the bloodiest fights of the Revolution. The battle left most of the Mohawk Valley in American hands.

Brant and his warriors sought to drive the Americans out by raiding and burning settlements and driving away livestock. Horrible massacres occurred on both sides. Throughout the valley people began to speak of "Monster Brant," although many of the atrocities may have been the work of pro-British Rangers who were operating in the same region. During the same period, pro-American forces launched similar raids against villages of Brant's Iroquois followers. The civilian populations on both sides were terrorized and demoralized.

The tragic outcome of this campaign came in 1779 when General George Washington sent a force of 4,000 troops to subdue the Iroquois. The Americans won a battle at Newtown in southern New York, then marched through Iroquois country, completing the devastation of homes, crops, and livestock.

Prior to the American Revolution, Brant had foreseen that if the colonists were victorious, they would swarm into Iroquois country in numbers. He, therefore, supported the British against the Americans. He hoped that if the British won the war, a sovereign Indian state, perhaps with himself as its leader, could be established in the lands west of the Allegheny Mountains. After the British were defeated and the war had ended, Brant moved west into Canada, where the British granted the Mohawks land along the Grand River in Ontario.

After 1785, Brant governed peacefully over the new Mohawk settlement from an elegant estate he established there. He devoted himself to promoting the welfare of the community and to religious translation and missionary activities. He also worked to secure peace between the United States and frontier tribes, but his influence was never the same. For the rest of his life, Brant struggled with a conflict of loyalties. His true loyalties were with the Iroquois although he clung to his belief that the British were valuable allies in the struggle to protect Indian interests. In the years following the American Revolution, his allegiance to the British aroused suspicion among many native people. Consequently, the British felt free to abandon many of their promises to his people for land and sovereignty. Yet they tried to maintain his loyalty, and at his death Joseph Brant was still drawing pay as a colonel in the British army.

ہ ہ ہ ہ

Red Jacket
Seneca orator
1756?–1830

"I am an orator! I was born an orator!" said Red Jacket when asked about his wartime activities. The words were appropriate, for Red Jacket's talents were not as a soldier, but rather as a negotiator, a statesman, and as an eloquent spokesman for the Seneca people and for all of the members of the Iroquois Confederacy.

Red Jacket was born about 1756 in what is now western New York state. His original Seneca name was Otetiani. But he took the name Sagoyewatha, meaning "he keeps them awake," when he became a sachem, a peace chief who managed the tribe's civil affairs. Little is known about Red Jacket until the time of the American Revolutionary War, when along with the rest of the Seneca nation he fought on the side of the British. It was during this war that he took the English name Red Jacket, in recognition of the red coat that he wore while serving with the British.

Although Red Jacket became an advocate of peace with Americans, he was opposed to the growth of white settlement on Indian lands. One of his earliest recorded speeches was delivered on this subject in 1797. In the speech, he compares native land holdings to a small island, and he pictures expansion into the territories as a great flood:

> We stand a small island in the bosom of the great waters. We are encircled— we are encompassed. The evil spirit rides upon the [wind], and the waters are disturbed. They rise, they press upon us, and the waves will settle over us, and we shall disappear forever. Who then lives to mourn us? None. What marks our extermination? Nothing. We are mingled with the common elements.

Red Jacket was also a forceful opponent of the spread of Christianity to native peoples. One of his most famous speeches was delivered on this subject in 1805. A young missionary had come to convert the Senecas. After the missionary had finished talking, Red Jacket began the following speech, which reviews the history of white people in America:

> Your forefathers crossed the great water and landed on the island [North America]. Their numbers were small. They found friends and not enemies. They told us they had fled from their own country for fear of wicked men, and had come here to enjoy their religion. They asked for a small seat. We took pity on them, granted their request, and they sat down amongst us.

Red Jacket then went on to the issue of religion:

> Brother: Continue to listen.... We understand that your religion is written in a book. If it was intended for us as well as you, why has not the Great Spirit given to us . . . the knowledge of that book, with the means to understand it rightly? We only know what you tell us about it. How shall we know when to believe, being so often deceived by white people?
>
> Brother: You say there is but one way to worship and serve the Great Spirit. If there is but one religion, why do you white people differ so much about it? Why not all agreed, as you can all read the book?
>
> Brother: We do not understand these things. We are told that your religion was given to your forefathers, and has been handed down from father to son. We also have a religion, which was given to our forefathers, and has been handed down to us their children. We worship in that way. It teaches us to be thankful for all the favors we receive, to love each other, and to be united. We never quarrel about religion.
>
> Brother: We do not wish to destroy your religion, or take it from you. We only want to enjoy our own.

Over the years, Red Jacket often spoke about Christianity and the behavior of non-Indians. One of his most famous speeches on the subject, from around 1811, uses pointed satire as well as eloquence. In the speech he refers to the city of Buffalo, New York, which was near where he lived at the time:

Perhaps you think we are ignorant and uninformed. Go, then, and teach the whites. Select, for example, the people of Buffalo. We will be spectators, and remain silent. Improve their morals and refine their habits. Make them less disposed to cheat Indians. Make the whites generally less inclined to make Indians drunk, and to take from them their lands. Let us know the tree by the blossoms, and the blossoms by their fruit. When this shall be made clear to our minds we may be more willing to listen to you. But until then we must be allowed to follow the religion of our ancestors.

Throughout a long career as a leader and spokesman for the Iroquois people, Red Jacket worked to promote Indian unity, to halt land sales to whites, and to prevent further white invasion of Indian lands. By the end of his life, he foresaw a sad future for his people. On the final day of his life, he spoke about his feelings in one of his most moving speeches:

I am about to leave you, and when I am gone and my warning shall no longer be heard or regarded, the craft and the avarice of the white man will prevail. Many winters I have [withstood] the storm, but I am an aged tree, and can stand no longer. My leaves are fallen, my branches are withered, and I am shaken by every breeze. Soon my aged trunk will [fall to the ground], and the foot of the exulting foe of the Indian may be placed upon it with safety; for I leave none who will be able to avenge such an injury. Think not I mourn for myself. I go to join the spirits of my fathers, where age cannot come; but my heart fails when I think of my people, who are soon to be scattered and forgotten.

છ છ છ છ

Tecumseh
Shawnee war chief, political leader, and orator
1768–1813

Imagine a great nation, independent of the United States, stretching down the middle of the continent from Canada to the Gulf of Mexico. That was the goal of Tecumseh, one of the greatest statesmen and warriors in American Indian history. But before such a nation could take shape, Tecumseh was killed in battle and the opportunity for an Indian union passed.

Tecumseh emerged as an important leader during the time when the American nation was expanding outward from the original thirteen colonies into the region called the Old Northwest—roughly the lands between the Great Lakes on the north and the Ohio River Valley on the south. To land-hungry American settlers heading westward, the Old Northwest was a huge untapped resource waiting to be claimed. But to Native Americans living there, it was home, as it had been for generations. They resisted the American invaders, sometimes with success. As the number of settlers grew, the conflict became more bitter and the Indian situation more desperate.

Tecumseh was born in western Ohio in 1768 during this troubled time. Frontier warfare shattered his early years. His father, a Shawnee war chief; a brother; and his adoptive father were killed by white soldiers. His mother, shocked and overwhelmed, left him and his brothers and sisters to be raised by their older sister.

While he was still very young, Tecumseh showed great military abilities. In 1782, at the age of fourteen, he fought in his first battle, on the side of the British in the American Revolution. During the 1780s and 1790s, he took part in various raids and skirmishes and was recognized among the Shawnee as an exceptional leader.

In spite of his unfriendliness toward whites, Tecumseh was known for his compassion toward prisoners. While still in his teens, he witnessed the torture of a white prisoner. He was horrified, and he spoke so forcefully and effectively against such practices that his fellow Shawnee never dared mistreat prisoners in his presence again. Even his white adversaries understood that his stand against cruelty was genuine, and they admired him for it. Perhaps it was this experience that showed him the power he could wield with words. Persuading with brilliant oratory became a essential part of his later activities.

In 1795, Tecumseh took an important stand opposing many other Indian leaders. Chiefs from across the Old Northwest had agreed to a treaty that turned over land to whites. Tecumseh refused to sign the treaty. Criticizing the chiefs who had signed, he said that they had no right to give away any land, because like the air and water, the land was held in common by all Indians, not by particular individuals or tribes.

This was one of the first times he spoke publicly about an idea that was to become his central theme—the idea of one unified Indian nation. In the next years, he used his oratorical skills to spread his idea among many different nations, from the Great Lakes to the Mississippi Valley to the Southeast. Tecumseh traveled great distances to draw together diverse Indian peoples. In numerous discussions and councils, Tecumseh urged tribes whose traditional ways of life were being destroyed to join in a unified political resistance to the white settlers and soldiers.

During this same period, Tecumseh's brother, Tenskwatawa, which means "The Open Door" or "I Am the Door," was emerging as an important Shawnee religious leader. Tenskwatawa, also called "the Prophet," preached that Indians should return to traditional ways, forgo old conflicts among tribes, and unite to reject white customs, including land deals, use of alcohol, and other corrupting influences. Because their goals were so similar, Tecumseh began to work with Tenskwatawa. Their movement began to gather strength. In 1808, the brothers founded a town in Indiana, Tippecanoe (or Prophetstown), where their followers gathered.

The governor of Indiana, William Henry Harrison, saw these developments as dangerous. He tried to undo the growing Indian alliance with clever treaties and outright trickery. Still, Tecumseh continued to persuade more tribal leaders to join the alliance. In 1811, Tecumseh set off on more travels to round up support, leaving Tenskwatawa at Prophetstown with firm warnings to avoid conflict with Harrison until he returned with more allies.

In November, with Tecumseh still away, Harrison brought a militia force to Prophetstown and accused the Indians of stealing. Indian leaders advised Tenskwatawa to attack the militia. Harrison's force retaliated, and Prophetstown was burned to the ground. The Indian alliance was badly shaken by the loss at Prophetstown. Tenskwatawa was discredited, and he fell into obscurity.

Tecumseh continued his efforts to build Indian unity. Along with other leaders, he knew that even if they were united, the Indians could never defeat the armies of the U.S. government. At this time, however, the War of 1812 was about to erupt between the U.S. and Great Britain. So Tecumseh gave his support to the British. He thought that a British victory would limit American expansion into Indian lands.

Tecumseh joined the British in southern Canada and assembled one of the most powerful fighting forces ever commanded by an American Indian. The Indian warriors played a vital role in the British capture of Detroit and 2,500 American soldiers stationed there. Tecumseh then accompanied the British into Ohio and tried to capture Fort Meigs, which was commanded by Tecumseh's old foe, William Henry Harrison. But in the end, Tecumseh and the British failed at Fort Meigs. After a series of American victories in the region, the British withdrew to Canada.

Although Tecumseh wanted to stay in Ohio and fight, he agreed to withdraw to keep the fighting forces together. Harrison followed in pursuit. On October 5, 1813, the armies met in a decisive battle along the Thames River in Ontario. Tecumseh directed much of the battle that day. His Indian forces fought bravely and well, but the British seemed to have lost their will to fight. After Tecumseh himself was killed, Harrison won a total victory.

With the death of Tecumseh, most Indian resistance in the Old Northwest ended. The defeated peoples were later forced to move to lands west of the Mississippi River. Yet Tecumseh's efforts to create a unified Indian nation are remembered as one of the most successful attempts to preserve the American Indian way of life on this continent.

Tecumseh was killed in 1813 at the Battle of the Thames in Ontario, Canada.

Sequoyah
Inventor of Cherokee writing system
*c.*1770–1843

Sequoyah succeeded in creating a Cherokee alphabet, or syllabary, at a time when others saw it as an impossible task. An impoverished farmer and hunter, he was never taught to read or write English. He spoke his native Cherokee, a language noted for its complexity. Yet he became obsessed with the idea of writing his native language and singlehandedly invented a method of setting down his words on paper. His invention gave the Cherokee the ability to communicate directly with each other in their own language across distance and time.

Sequoyah was born in the mountains of eastern Tennessee. His mother, a Cherokee woman by the name of Wur-teh, raised him in traditional Cherokee ways. His father was possibly Nathaniel Gist, a trader and soldier, but Sequoyah never knew him. Wur-teh managed to make a meager living for herself and her son by raising horses and dairy cattle on a few acres of land. Sequoyah never went to school and seems to have been a dreamy, solitary child with little interest in the usual competitive sports and games of Cherokee boys. Rather, his interests were in building things with his hands. When he was old enough, he helped with the farm work and began to hunt and trap to add to the family income.

At some point in his youth—perhaps in a hunting accident—he injured his leg and was left crippled. Some accounts say that he drank heavily for a brief period after he was crippled. Then he turned to a craft that fascinated him: working with silver. The Cherokee traditionally wore bracelets, buttons, buckles, and other such ornaments of silver, and Sequoyah began to fashion these items. He was very patient and attentive to detail, and he became a superb silversmith.

In spite of his lameness, Sequoyah served as a soldier in the U.S. Army in the Creek War of 1813–1814. For several years before then, he had been intrigued by the mysterious symbols that white people made on pieces of paper, which conveyed messages. During his time as a soldier, he became convinced that having a written language would open up many possibilities for Indians and provide them with opportunities. So he devoted himself to the task of inventing a practical, usable system for writing the Cherokee language.

Sequoyah first tried to design a symbol to represent each word in the Cherokee language. Before long he realized that this system wouldn't work, because he would need thousands of symbols. Then he tried to make a symbol for each different syllable sound that he could hear in the language. That approach was more promising, because there were far fewer different syllables to figure out. After years of studying his language, Sequoyah identified eighty-six separate sounds. He created a symbol, or character, to represent each sound he identified. Some of these characters were copied from English, Greek, or Hebrew letters he saw in books; others he made up. Now Sequoyah had a *syllabary*—a set of written symbols, or characters, in which each character represents the sound of a single syllable found in the language.

During the years when Sequoyah was working on his syllabary, many people who observed his avid interest in drawing odd-shaped symbols thought it was foolish. Worse yet, they thought he might be working black magic. He was shunned by friends and family alike during this difficult time. But he quickly won approval when in 1821 he demonstrated to Cherokee leaders that, using his method, even his young daughter could write and read their language. Sequoyah's system was easy to learn, and within a short time Cherokees everywhere were using it. Parts of the Bible were soon available in the new syllabary; a newspaper, the *Cherokee Phoenix*, was published in it; a tribal constitution was written down; letters were exchanged with faraway relatives.

Cherokee Alphabet.

D *a*	R *e*	T *i*	Ꮤ *o*	O *u*	i *v*
S *ga* Ꮝ *ka*	Ꮖ *ge*	Ꮩ *gi*	A *go*	J *gu*	E *gv*
Ꮚ *ha*	P *he*	Ꮀ *hi*	Ꮂ *ho*	Ꮁ *hu*	Ꮃ *hv*
W *la*	Ꮔ *le*	P *li*	G *lo*	M *lu*	Ꮅ *lv*
Ꮵ *ma*	Ꮉ *me*	H *mi*	Ꮿ *mo*	Y *mu*	
Ꮎ *na* Ꮏ *hna* Ᏽ *nah*	Ꮑ *ne*	Ꮕ *ni*	Z *no*	Ꮒ *nu*	Ꮏ *nv*
Ꮖ *qua*	Ꮙ *que*	Ꮤ *qui*	Ꮴ *quo*	Ꮵ *quu*	Ꮛ *quv*
Ꮳ *sa* Ꮝ *s*	Ꮞ *se*	Ꮖ *si*	Ꮩ *so*	Ꮝ *su*	R *sv*
Ꮬ *da* Ꮤ *ta*	Ꮪ *de* Ꮖ *te*	Ꮧ *di* Ꮨ *ti*	V *do*	S *du*	Ꮭ *dv*
Ꮦ *dla* Ꮤ *tla*	L *tle*	C *tli*	Ꮯ *tlo*	Ꮰ *tlu*	P *tlv*
Ꮳ *tsa*	Ꮴ *tse*	Ᏺ *tsi*	K *tso*	Ꮵ *tsu*	Ꮶ *tsv*
G *wa*	Ꮺ *we*	Ꮻ *wi*	Ꮼ *wo*	Ꮽ *wu*	Ꮾ *wv*
Ꮓ *ya*	B *ye*	Ꭼ *yi*	Ꮀ *yo*	Ꮘ *yu*	B *yv*

*An early printed chart showing the characters
Sequoyah created for his syllabary of the Cherokee language*

32

Sharing ideas and greetings across long distances was especially important to the Cherokee, because part of the tribe had been moved west to Arkansas. Sequoyah, too, moved to Arkansas, and later to Indian Territory (Oklahoma) to help spread the use of his writing system as a means of unifying and strengthening his people. His contributions made him a respected and important person among the Cherokee. He served as a tribal representative to the U.S. government in Washington in the continuing struggle over land rights. He was awarded a lifetime pension by the Cherokee National Council.

Sequoyah never lost his interest in Indian languages and the relationships among them. In later years, he also became interested in the story of the "lost Cherokee," a group who were believed to have traveled west half a century earlier and disappeared. Sequoyah hoped to find these people by seeking out some Cherokee speakers rumored to live in Mexico. In 1842, Sequoyah, by then an old man, set out for Mexico with a small band of followers. He is thought to have died in Mexico in the summer of 1843.

Sequoyah's genius with language and his years of careful labor on a syllabary produced a great and enduring gift to the Cherokee nation—written communication. Of the many tributes to him, the most fitting may be that the greatest tree that grows in America, the California giant redwood, known as the *sequoia*, was named in his honor.

ᏸ ᏸ ᏸ ᏸ

Sacagawea
Lemhi Shoshone interpreter
*c.*1786–1812?

"**S**acagawea reconciles all the Indians to our friendly intentions. A woman with a party of men is a token of peace." That is how William Clark, co-leader of the Lewis and Clark Expedition, described the principal contribution of the only woman to take part in their epic trek of exploration across the United States to reach the Pacific Ocean. As Meriwether Lewis put it, she was "the inspiration, the genius of the occasion."

Although she has become a subject of legends, history really knows Sacagawea only through a few scattered references, mainly in Clark's writings. But the sparse facts make clear that the exploring party had many reasons to honor her. At various times on the trip she served as diplomat, interpreter, guide, cook, and nurse. Once she even saved the expedition's journals and records from oblivion by plucking them out of an icy river when a canoe capsized. Sacagawea's store of knowledge and her survival skills were invaluable help to them all.

It is likely that Sacagawea was in her late teens when she slipped into the historical record. She was probably born in the Bitterroot Mountains of east-central Idaho. Her people were the Lemhi Shoshones, who traveled widely on horseback in search of game and useful wild plants. Her association with Lewis and Clark came about through a series of chance happenings.

One day when she was about thirteen, Sacagawea's Shoshone band encountered a raiding party from an enemy tribe, and she was kidnapped. Her captors sold or traded her to the Mandans, a tribe who lived along the Missouri River far from her homeland, in what became North Dakota. When she was about seventeen, she became the wife of a French-Canadian fur trader, Toussaint Charbonneau.

About the same time the U.S. government bought from France the vast territory known as the Louisiana Purchase. To learn more about the new lands, an expedition led by Clark and Lewis was organized. The explorers departed from St. Louis, Missouri, in May 1804, and headed up the Missouri River. They stopped for the winter at the Mandan encampment in North Dakota. There they met Charbonneau and hired him as an interpreter. When the party left in the spring, Charbonneau brought along Sacagawea and their infant son, Jean-Baptiste, nicknamed Pomp.

Surely Sacagawea hoped to visit her Shoshone relatives as the expedition pushed westward. With little Pomp on her back on a cradleboard, she set out on the journey that would be many hundreds of miles. As the expedition went along, she proved to be a significant help—certainly more than Charbonneau, who was rather clumsy and easily panicked. The party had to cross the Rocky Mountains and find the Columbia River. The leaders had almost no information about what lay in the middle of their route, but that area was Sacagawea's homeland.

Sacagawea soon earned everyone's respect for her calmness and courage in the face of hardships. Like most of the party, she was usually on foot. Sometimes she would walk with William Clark and, using a combination of English, French, and sign language, explain lore she knew about the places and things they passed.

Early in the trip Sacagawea began to supplement the party's regular rations with edible wild plants. Not only did these foods make meals more interesting, but they also added vital nutrients to their diet and insured the travelers' good health. She also knew something about medicinal plants, and which plants to avoid because they were poisonous. Contrary to many stories about her, Sacagawea did not serve as a guide. At a few critical points along the way, however, she identified important landmarks and steered the party in the right direction. She also could recognize moccasin prints. From distinctive patterns in fresh prints, she could tell the moccasin wearer's tribe, and thus who might be nearby.

Sacagawea's mere presence in the group, especially with Pomp, was a signal of good intentions to Indians that they met. She may be credited with the fact that the party never found itself in a hostile situation. She knew how to communicate with signs, and she was able to speak the Mandan and Shoshone languages. Sometimes through a long chain of interpreters, Lewis and Clark were able to communicate with other tribes as well.

It turned out that Sacagawea was about the best possible person to accompany the party in Shoshone country. They badly needed help in getting across the Continental Divide, especially horses to get over the mountains. In

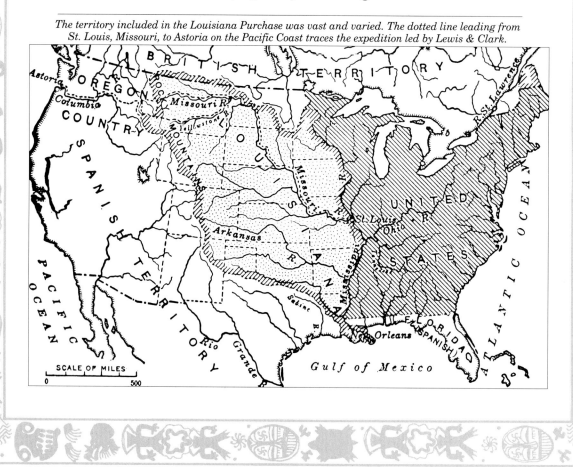

The territory included in the Louisiana Purchase was vast and varied. The dotted line leading from St. Louis, Missouri, to Astoria on the Pacific Coast traces the expedition led by Lewis & Clark.

a stroke of extraordinary good fortune, the party encountered Sacagawea's brother, Cameahwait, who had become a chief. It had been five years since brother and sister had seen each other, and their reunion was very emotional. Although she knew Cameahwait was unfriendly towards whites, Sacagawea repeatedly asked for his assistance for her friends. Eventually Cameahwait provided horses, supplies, and guides to help the explorers complete their journey over the mountains and down to the Columbia River.

In November 1805, the expedition reached the Pacific Ocean. Their mission complete, they turned back toward St. Louis, taking a somewhat different route. Sacagawea and Charbonneau accompanied them as far as the Mandan town in North Dakota.

What became of Sacagawea is unclear. It is known that in 1809 Clark brought the Charbonneau family to St. Louis, where they were settled on a farm. Clark was fond of Pomp and arranged for his education. A note in Clark's papers suggests that Sacagawea lived only a few years more. Other accounts, however, indicate that she returned to the Shoshones to live much longer, possibly to as much as a hundred years old. The real story of her death will probably remain one of history's secrets.

ða ða ða ða

Seathl
Duwamish chief and orator
c.1788–1866

Seattle, Washington, is the largest city in the Americas to be named for an American Indian. It is named in honor of a chief who showed great friendship for white people. He was also a great orator.

His name was Seathl, or sometimes Sealth, or even See-yat. (Settlers had a hard time pronouncing his name correctly, especially the sound at the end of it.) Seathl's father's people, the Suquamish, and his mother's, the Duwamish, were two allied groups who lived in villages along the deep inlet off of the Pacific Ocean now called Puget Sound. They were fishers and hunters, and, like people of other Northwest Coast cultures, they had wonderfully efficient dugout canoes that they used for travel, fishing, and warfare.

Seathl was very young when in 1792 the "white-winged bird ship" *Discovery* of the English navigator George Vancouver came to the region. Vancouver was on an expedition to survey and map the Pacific Coast of North America. Before that time, Northwest Coast Indians had had almost no contact with whites. During Seathl's life, all that changed. His brief experience with the strangers impressed the boy greatly, and perhaps that is why Seathl was so ready in later life to advocate peaceful, tolerant relations with those who settled nearby.

When he was still a young man, Seathl inherited his father's chieftainship. Not long after that he was named principal chief of a confederation of the Suquamish, Duwamish, and other groups. He earned this position because of his successful leadership in warfare against other tribes in the area. He held the position for the rest of his life, although he never again led a fighting force.

Among the earliest Europeans to enter the area were French Catholic missionaries, who came in the 1830s. Seathl was very impressed with their beliefs and converted to Christianity, taking the baptismal name Noah. He started the practice of twice-daily prayer services among his people, which they continued until after his death.

The city named for Chief Seathl is today a thriving cultural and commercial metropolis. Mt. Rainier can be seen in the background.

Seathl was considered a venerable, dignified elder leader by the time the first permanent white settlement was established in his part of Puget Sound, in 1851. He welcomed the newcomers, who at Seathl's suggestion set up a trading post on the east side of the Sound, in what is now the heart of the city of Seattle. The settlement quickly began to prosper and grow.

In 1852, the settlement's name, Alki Point, was changed to Seattle, a version of Seathl's name. More and more people began coming to the region, and within a few years the relationship between the settlers and the Indians deteriorated. Elsewhere native peoples were being relocated onto reservations, and in late 1854 several local tribes developed a plan to drive the settlers out. They regarded with suspicion Seathl's continued view that friendship was the right path. In January 1855, Governor Isaac Stevens of the Washington Territory summoned the Puget Sound tribes together and proposed a treaty that would take control of their lands and move them onto a reservation.

Sadly realizing that these changes appeared inevitable, Seathl was the first to sign the Treaty of Port Elliott. Despite the treaty, trouble soon broke out between the settlers and a combination of native groups from eastern Washington and some coastal peoples. The conflict lasted for several years. Throughout this period, Seathl and most of his followers counseled peace. They moved to a reservation on the western side of Puget Sound. Seathl lived in a large "community house," a wooden building nearly 60 x 900 feet, called Old Man House. There he spent the remainder of his life.

Seathl was a tall, strong man, with a clear, resonating voice that could be understood by everyone in a large group of people. His great ability as a orator is apparent in a famous speech that he made to Governor Stevens in 1854 when the governor visited Seattle. Seathl's Dawamish words were interpreted and written down by a white listener. While the translation may not exactly represent what he said, the speaker's eloquence shines through. Here is some of that speech:

Every part of this soil is sacred in the estimation of my people. Every hillside, every valley, every plain and grove, has been hallowed by some sad or happy event in days long vanished. The very dust upon which you now stand responds more lovingly to their footsteps than to yours, because it is rich with the blood of our ancestors and our bare feet are conscious of the sympathetic touch. . . . When the last Red Man shall have perished, and the memory of my tribe shall have become a myth among the White Men, these shores will swarm with the invisible dead of my tribe, and when your children's children think themselves alone in the field, the store, the shop, upon the highway, or in the silence of the pathless woods, they will not be alone. At night when the streets of your cities and villages are silent and you think them deserted, they will throng with the returning hosts that once filled and still love this beautiful land. The White Man will never be alone. Let him be just and deal kindly with my people, for the dead are not powerless. Dead, did I say? There is no death, only a change of worlds.

Losing the Land:
Indian Removals and the Dawes Act

Beginning in the 1500s with the earliest European settlements in North America, native peoples were driven off their land. Initially, disease played an enormous role in this process. Many American Indians died in epidemics soon after their first contact with whites. This was because they had no natural immunity to deadly European plagues such as smallpox. Indians were also forced off their land by more deliberate means, notably warfare. Again and again, Indians resisted invasion with force. But, in the end, the Indians were nearly always outnumbered.

In the eighteenth century, another kind of displacement from the land entered the picture. Especially after the American Revolution, many tribes were pressured with laws, treaties, threats, and other strong-arm tactics to move from their homelands. During the nineteenth century, especially the period from about 1815 to 1850, these Indian "removals" reached their peak. The uprooting and relocating of whole native populations became part of federal government policy.

In 1803, President Thomas Jefferson doubled the size of the United States when he authorized buying the Louisiana Purchase, a huge territory extending westward from the Mississippi River. To people interested in expanding the American frontier, the new territory seemed like a good place to put Indians. Some used the excuse that it was right and natural that Indian "savagery" should vanish as white "civilization" progressed. But many others just wanted to take what the Indians had.

Land-hungry white Americans felt blocked by the presence of native peoples in areas that they wanted to occupy. The land east of the Mississippi provided many opportunities, they said. The eastern land would be very good to farm and mine and build upon. Would-be homesteaders proposed removing the Indians to the West. Few people guessed how soon settlers would fill the East and want to take over the West too.

Andrew Jackson, a war hero who was elected president in 1828, was one of the principal advocates of Indian removal. He, like many other Americans, believed that to be strong the United States had to continue expanding into Indian territory. They felt that to help accomplish this, Indians should either become like white citizens, or they should be required to leave so as not to interfere with growth. A rising tide of anti-Indian racism added to this desire to get Indians out of the way.

Andrew Jackson

Other people supported removal as the best way of saving Indians from destruction. They saw that Indians suffered terribly from disease, alcoholism, and poverty when they came into contact with whites. These "friends" of Indians, as they called themselves, thought that if Indians were removed beyond the reach of white frontiersmen, they might learn to adopt white ways without suffering the bad effects of contact.

Whatever justification was given, removal meant exile. Various treaties requiring removal were negotiated. Then in 1830, President Jackson signed into law the Indian Removal Act, setting off a decade of the most intensive removals. Eventually the act was used to evict and send west more than 100,000 Indians.

A large part of this total were members of the "Five Civilized Tribes"—the Cherokees, Choctaws, Chickasaws, Muscogees (Creek), and Seminoles—who for many generations had lived in the Southeastern United States. Although some tribes were beginning to adopt European ways, all five tribes were eventually forced to leave their homelands for Indian Territory, the area that is today the state of Oklahoma.

The Cherokee, a nation in their own right, had a thriving economy, tax-supported schools, a newspaper, a mounted police force, and a government modeled after that of the United States. The problem was that they had prosperous farms on fertile lands, which whites wanted, especially after gold was discovered there too. When the state of Georgia passed a bill that allowed division of Cherokee territory in Georgia into parcels of land for white settlement, the Cherokee Nation filed two lawsuits against the state. The ruling of Supreme Court Justice John Marshall favored Cherokee rights to disregard Georgia state laws. Unfortunately, Georgia disregarded Marshall's ruling and President Jackson did nothing to enforce it. Muscogees in Alabama were removed in chains. Choctaws were forced from Mississippi in winter without proper clothing or provisions. Also in winter, Black Hawk, a Sauk chief, and his people were forced from their village in Illinois and marched west into Iowa. In 1835, the Seminole in Florida faced a similar fate. Although they fought guerrilla-style warfare to avoid removal, most were driven west.

By 1838, all efforts to stall the removal of the Cherokee had been blocked. Federal troops began brutally rounding up and imprisoning them. During the next winter, the Cherokees were forced to travel westward under armed guard. Of approximately 16,000 Cherokees who were removed, perhaps 4,000 died along the way of starvation, exhaustion, and the cold. Thousands more died soon after they arrived. This forced march is called the "Trail of Tears."

This painting titled "The Trail of Tears" by Robert Lindaur captures the agony and tragedy of Indian removal west.

Once in the newly established Indian Territory, many Indians endured terrible deprivation because the federal government had no plan for dealing with them. Indians native to the area often reacted with violence to the new arrivals from the East. Feuding and factionalism weakened tribes from within. There were decades of misery, during which Indians were herded onto ever smaller reservations only to find their land rights again under attack by floods of land-hungry settlers moving westward. It became clear even to government policy-makers that "the Indian problem," as it was called, was far from solved.

By the 1880s, a plan to dissolve Indian tribes and end communal land holdings surfaced. In 1887, it was made into a federal law called the General Allotment Act or the Dawes Act. Traditionally, most native peoples believed that land was held in common by all the members of the community that occupied it. The Dawes Act sought to end that system. It broke up reservations into allotments, or individual plots of land (usually 160 acres) to be granted to individual Indian families. Indians who received allotments could be made U.S. citizens.

The plan was supposed to encourage Indians to become independent small farmers, just like white people. As property owners, Indians were supposed to learn to look out for their own private interests, not tribal interests. They were supposed to give up their Indian ways and melt into the American mainstream.

Some sponsors of the Dawes Act thought they were finally doing the right thing to help Indians, but the act actually promoted the breakdown of tribal society and loss of land. Allotment tended to scatter individuals and families, and thus to cut the community ties that had helped people to get through the worst times. And the plan to turn all Indians into farmers did not work. For many native people accustomed to hunting, farming was not part of their cultural background. Private ownership of land seemed a strange, selfish idea. Much of the allotted land was not suitable for farming, or it went to people who were disabled, too old, or too young to farm. Most Indians had no money to buy seed and tools anyway.

An objective of the Dawes Act was to encourage Indians to become farmers, as they are depicted in this painting by Frederick Remington.

Further, the Dawes Act speeded up Indian land loss. Indeed, some observers said the real motivation behind the act was to get control of more Indian land into white hands. It made available for sale large areas of leftover unallotted tribal land, which non-Indians bought up at bargain prices. Some land was simply seized by settlers, without any pretense of a legal transfer. Under some conditions, Indians were encouraged to sell their allotments, and many did. Problems surfaced regarding rules for inheriting allotments, which also led to transfers of land to whites.

The effect of all this was that in less than fifty years, Indian holdings shrank from 138 million to 48 million acres. Much of the remaining land was undesirable desert or semidesert. By 1934, two-thirds of the Indians had no land at all or not enough to provide even the most meager living.

Removal and allotment were both attempts to control Indian destiny that sprang from alliances of greed and misguided humanitarian impulses. It was not until 1934, nearly half a century after the Dawes Act, that the Indian Reorganization Act would attempt to correct the failures of the Dawes Act. The new reform legislation ended the policy of allotment and the selling off of unallotted reservation lands. Finally, Indians' chances for keeping what little land they still held began to improve. But lasting damage had already been done. These early government policies of removal and allotment still affect the lives of Indian people today.

ða ða ða ða

Osceola
Seminole patriot and resistance leader
*c.*1804–1838

I t has been said that when federal government officials called Seminole leaders together to sign a treaty giving up their land, most silently refused to touch the pen. But Osceola strode to the table and in angry contempt plunged his hunting knife through the paper.

The year was 1835, and the U.S. government was beginning to mount its strongest campaign to remove Seminoles from Florida and relocate them west of the Mississippi River. Osceola was recognized as the Seminoles' head war chief. His determination and abilities made him their acknowledged leader in their fight to resist relocation. Ancestors of the Seminoles came from many tribes. The word Seminole is derived from a Muscogee (Creek) word *simonoli* meaning "runaway." In the eighteenth and early nineteenth centuries, various peoples, mainly Muscogees, left their homelands in Georgia, Alabama, Mississippi, and South Carolina and migrated southward into the Spanish territory of Florida. Most were fleeing wars or outbreaks of disease. By the early 1800s, the Indians were being joined by escaped black slaves, who settled among them, sometimes married Indians, and became a part of Seminole society.

Osceola was born in a Muscogee Indian village near the Tallapoosa River in northern Alabama between 1803–1804. He moved with his mother to Seminole country in northern Florida when he was about ten, after the Creek War of 1813–1814. As a teenager, he may have fought with the Seminoles against the United States in the First Seminole War of 1817–1818. Although the conflict was named for the Seminole Indians, in the words of General Sidney Thomas Jesup, it began as ". . . a Negro and not an Indian War."

The Seminoles had long offered protection to escaped slaves who, over the years, had settled among them. By 1816, Seminoles and slaves had joined forces to resist white encroachment into their territory. U.S. troops invaded Florida to wipe out Seminole resistance and "restore the stolen negroes . . . to their rightful owners." In July 1816, U.S. troops massacred 270 Black Seminoles who had taken over a British fortress on the Apalachicola River in Florida. The incident, which remained a secret for twenty years, was followed by other "search and destroy" missions aimed at crushing Seminole resistance and stopping the ever-growing influence of independent, armed, free blacks in the Seminole nation.

When Spain ceded Florida to the United States in 1819, U.S. military operations increased. Still, resistance among the Seminoles and their black

The Seminoles under Osceola's expert leadership fought bravely to avoid the U.S. government's attempts to remove them from their homeland in Florida.

allies remained strong. By 1823, however, the Seminoles were forced to accept a treaty that gave millions of acres of their land to the U.S. government and restricted the Seminoles to an area in southern Florida. Life there was much worse than it had been in the north. The land was not good for farming or hunting, and many people began to feel the pinch of hunger. Professional slave catchers continued to hound the Seminoles for runaway slaves. Resentment grew. According to one story, Osceola's wife, who was the daughter of a black slave and thus considered a slave herself, was among those seized and shipped away. This wrenching experience is said to have sparked a deep hatred for white people in Osceola, and he swore he would get revenge.

In 1830, the Indian Removal Act was signed into law by Andrew Jackson, who was then the U.S. president. The Act called for the removal of many Indian tribes, including the Seminoles, far to the west. Whites were eager to move on to and farm the lands occupied by Indians.

A few Seminole leaders signed the Treaty of Payne's Landing in 1832, agreeing to relocate the tribe in three years. Most Seminoles, however, did not accept the plan set forth in the treaty. Prominent among those who resisted was Osceola.

When the three years were about up, in 1835, the Indian agent, General Wiley Thompson, summoned tribal leaders together to sign a treaty confirming that the Seminoles would depart. It was then that Osceola reportedly made his feelings clear by slashing the treaty document with his knife. After a quarrel, Thompson had Osceola arrested and imprisoned. He was soon released, but the episode only deepened Osceola's anger and determination.

Osceola and his followers began a highly effective guerrilla campaign of resistance. Rather than fighting the U.S. army in force, they would suddenly attack and then retreat into the swamps. On one such raid, Osceola got revenge when he and his warriors killed Wiley Thompson as he sat at dinner. In retaliation, more army troops were sent into the area in an effort to capture Osceola and subdue the Seminoles. The conflict, which is remembered as the

Second Seminole War, lasted from 1835 to 1842. It proved to be extremely expensive for the U.S. government, both in terms of money and in lives lost. In the end, the government objective of subduing the Seminoles was only partly accomplished.

Osceola was plainly the most important of the Seminole war chiefs. He earned respect among Indians and non-Indians alike for his successful tactics. The U.S. army, on the other hand, was commanded by a succession of generals who were sent in to capture Osceola and "wind up the war." Several generals tried and then lost their jobs because they failed. Finally one succeeded, by resorting to treachery. In late 1837, General Thomas Jesup proposed that Osceola come to peace talks at St. Augustine, Florida. When Osceola appeared under a white flag of truce, Jesup had him seized. This outrage raised many protests from the American public, but to no effect.

Many Seminoles, including Osceola, were first imprisoned at St. Augustine. A short time later, Osceola was sent to a prison at Fort Moultrie, South Carolina. There his health went downhill very rapidly, and he died a few months later in January 1838. Whether the cause of his decline was disease, poison, mistreatment, or grief is unclear. He refused the services of the white doctor, George Weedon, who saw him in prison. Perhaps something about Weedon made Osceola wary.

Weedon, it turned out, was Wiley Thompson's brother-in-law. After Osceola's death, Weedon removed Osceola's head. He reportedly used it to frighten his three small sons into good behavior. Later it was displayed in a museum until the building was destroyed by fire in 1866.

More of the Second Seminole War was fought from time to time during the next four years, but without Osceola's leadership the Seminole spirit was diminished, and many Indians were killed. In 1842, 4,500 Seminole survivors were removed and sent to Indian Territory in what is today the state of Oklahoma. Hundreds of others stayed hidden in the swamps and continued the resistance. Their descendants still live in Florida today.

Ely Samuel Parker
Seneca chief and
Commissioner of Indian Affairs
1828–1895

Shortly before Ely Parker was born in 1828, his mother had a dream of a rainbow across a winter's sky. It connected the Seneca village where she lived with a white settlement nearby. An elder told her that the dream was a prophecy: "A son shall be born to you who will be distinguished among his nation as a peacemaker . . . he will be a wise white man, but he will never desert his Indian people, nor lay down his sachem's horn as a great chief. His name will reach from the east to the west, from north to south, as great among his Indian family and the pale-faces." Ely Parker was to live up to this prophecy in all respects.

Parker grew up in western New York state. His mother made sure that he was well educated in both white and Indian ways. She sent him to a school to learn English, mathematics, and geography. But she also taught him about the Seneca people and about his famous ancestors, among them Red Jacket, the famous orator. Learning English was difficult for Ely, but he mastered it, and by the age of fourteen, he was acting as a scribe and translator for the Seneca chiefs.

For most of his youth, Parker divided his time between his education and assisting the chiefs in their dealings with non-Indians. While still a teenager, he went on several missions to Washington, D.C., to try to persuade the federal government to stop threatening to remove the Senecas from their lands. In the course of these visits, he met with senators, cabinet members, and even the President of the United States.

During this period he met a young lawyer, Lewis Henry Morgan. Morgan was deeply interested in the Senecas, as well as the other Indian nations that were collectively called the Iroquois. In later years, Morgan became known as "the father of American anthropology." Parker began teaching Morgan about the Iroquois, and he served as Morgan's guide and interpreter, introducing him to elders and other important members of the Seneca nation.

The result of this collaboration was a book that listed Morgan as author, but that was partly written by Parker. At the time, it was the most carefully researched study of native people ever written. This widely respected work influenced the way people thought about culture and society for years to come.

During this period Parker began studying to become a lawyer. But because he was not a U.S. citizen the state of New York refused to grant him a license to practice law. Blocked in this career, Parker became instead a successful civil engineer, working at first for the state of New York and later for the U.S. government.

In recognition of his service to the Seneca nation, the Senecas named Parker a grand sachem (civil chief). At the time, he was only twenty-three years old. He took the name Donehogawa, which means "Open Door." The name was appropriate, for Parker was to be the door through which the Senecas and non-Indians would communicate. In 1857, he helped argue a case before the U.S. Supreme Court that led to a ruling protecting Tonawanda Senecas against eviction from their lands in New York. And in 1858, he helped negotiate an agreement that assured them a permanent right to their lands.

In 1861, when the American Civil War began, Parker tried to join the Union army, but because he was Indian and not a citizen, he was not allowed. "The fight must be settled by the white men alone," he was told. "Go home, cultivate your farm, and we will settle our own troubles among ourselves without any Indian aid."

For a while, Parker was a farmer, but he continued to try to get into the army. In 1863, he finally received a captain's commission and was sent to join the forces under the command of General Ulysses Grant. Parker started out working as an engineer, but because of his legal training and his superior writing skills he was soon assigned to Grant's headquarters staff.

Grant came to rely heavily on Parker and appointed him as his military secretary and chief assistant. Parker wrote reports, issued orders, and helped Grant with correspondence. He served during several major campaigns, and he was present for the surrender of the Confederate forces at Appomattox. It was there that Parker performed his most famous service of the war. After Grant and Confederate General Robert E. Lee had finished discussing the terms of the surrender, Parker wrote out the official documents that put an end to the fighting.

During the Civil War, Parker served as General Ulysses S. Grant's chief assistant and military secretary. Parker is the fourth man from the right; Grant, the nineth.

After the war, Parker, still on Grant's staff, proposed a comprehensive plan for a permanent settling of differences between the U.S. government and native people in the West. His plan was not adopted, but Parker became known as an expert voice on Indian affairs within the government.

In 1868, Grant was elected President, and he appointed Parker as Commissioner of Indian Affairs. He was the first American Indian to hold that post. As Commissioner, Parker pursued many of the policies that he had proposed earlier. He worked to establish reservations where Indian land and interests would be protected and Indians would receive an education that would prepare them to survive in a world dominated by non-Indians. Perhaps Ely Parker's most important action as Commissioner of Indian Affairs was the removal of corrupt officials and the hiring of office staff and field agents who were committed to protecting the interests of native peoples.

But in the course of making reforms, Parker made enemies as well. In 1871, one of these enemies struck back. A wealthy merchant who had unsuccessfully opposed Parker's policies in the past brought charges of fraud and misconduct in office against Parker. Parker was completely cleared by a congressional committee, but the attack on his character hurt him deeply. In the same year, Congress also passed a law that severely limited his authority as Commissioner. Parker decided to resign his position and leave Washington. He had held the post for just two years, but during those years he had brought relative peace to the West and had introduced policies that were just and supportive for native peoples.

For the remainder of his life, Parker was a businessman, an investor, and an official of the New York City Police Department. Most importantly, he continued to work on behalf of the Iroquois people as a consultant and lecturer. He died in 1895 at his home in Fairfield, Connecticut.

àª àª àª àª

The Sand Creek Massacre

An American flag flew in the November morning over the Indians camped beside the Sand Creek in eastern Colorado. Three years before, it had been a gift to the Southern Cheyenne chief Black Kettle from the U.S. Commissioner of Indian Affairs, Colonel A.B. Greenwood. The two had just signed a peace treaty. Greenwood said that as long as the flag waved above them, no soldiers would ever fire on Black Kettle or his followers. This promise, like so many others made to native people, was soon broken.

In the fall of 1864, tensions were high in the Colorado Territory. For years there had been a spiraling series of violent clashes between the settlers and native peoples. But not all the region's natives agreed that they should war against the settlers invading their homeland. Black Kettle, one of forty-four Cheyenne peace chiefs, was at Sand Creek in response to an invitation from Colorado governor John Evans. He and a band of Cheyennes and Arapahos had come to nearby Fort Lyon, intending to show that they were willing to submit to U.S. military authority. The commander of Fort Lyon directed Black Kettle and his partially disarmed band to make camp at a site along the Sand Creek, forty miles north of the fort. He promised that they would be safe there.

Colonel John Chivington, however, had different ideas. He was the commander of the Colorado Territory's military forces, which were not part of the regular U.S. army. He had recently formed the Colorado Third Cavalry, a unit made up of an odd assortment of short-term volunteers.

Chivington and Governor Evans agreed on a policy of attacking Cheyenne and Arapaho villages whenever and wherever any excuse could be found to do so. When Chivington heard that there were six hundred Cheyennes and Arapahos camped just a short distance from the thinly guarded Fort Lyon, he saw his excuse. He ordered the Colorado Third Cavalry, which had not yet seen any military action, to march from Denver to Fort Lyon, where they joined part of the Colorado First Cavalry. Chivington was now leading a force of 1,200 men equipped with pistols, carbines, and several cannons.

The morning of November 29, 1864, they fired on the Indians without warning. At first Black Kettle and two other chiefs, White Antelope (Cheyenne) and Left Hand (Arapaho), tried to calm their people and convince the attackers of their peaceful intentions. Black Kettle waved his American flag, and White Antelope and Left Hand stood with their arms folded, proclaiming that they would not fight. None of this made a difference. White Antelope and Left Hand were shot dead.

The attack became a massacre. The soldiers, in a frenzy, tried to kill everyone that they could, including old people, women, and children. Chivington ordered his artillery units to fire directly into the camp; and as people fled soldiers pursued them on horseback and cut them down with sabers. Many of the soldiers mutilated the bodies of their dead victims and took away body parts as trophies.

No one knows for sure how many people died at Sand Creek that day. The troops who conducted the attack were mostly inexperienced, poorly trained, and, according to many accounts, drunk. Perhaps as a result, many of the Indians at the encampment, including Black Kettle himself, were able to escape. By nightfall, the troops withdrew, and the survivors, some of them badly wounded, made their way on foot to a Cheyenne hunting camp fifty miles away.

Throughout human history, violent attacks like this have seldom gone unanswered, and so it was with Sand Creek. In the weeks and months that followed, word of the massacre spread among the native people of the region. The news stiffened the resolve of many Cheyenne, Arapaho, and Sioux people to resist further white invasion of their lands. Many stopped listening to Black Kettle and other chiefs who argued for making peace with whites. By January 1865, an alliance of Cheyennes, Arapahos, and Sioux was attacking settlers, wagon trains, and forts. They ripped out telegraph wires, forced the abandonment of supply routes, and caused panic and food shortages in Denver. The war in the West would be at its most intense levels for the next twenty-five years—until its tragic end at Wounded Knee in 1890—and surely some of the bravery and determination displayed by native people during that period was the direct result of their memories of what happened at Sand Creek.

In the immediate aftermath of the massacre, Chivington and his troops were hailed as heroes throughout Colorado. They were cheered in parades and other public appearances; newspapers praised their victory; approving citizens of Denver nicknamed the troops "the Bloody Third." As details of the incident came to be known around the country, however, much of the public reacted with horror and disgust. Three separate military and civilian investigations of the incident were conducted, and all of them condemned it. Chivington was forced to resign from the military and to abandon his hoped-for political career. He lived the rest of his life in obscurity and disgrace, but neither he nor any of his troops were ever brought to trial for their actions that day.

The Sand Creek Massacre

Black Kettle continued to be a forceful advocate for peace with non-Indians. In 1867, he was one of the signers of the Treaty of Medicine Lodge in which the Cheyennes, Arapahos, and some Comanches and Kiowas were assigned reservations within Indian Territory. Although the months that followed saw some frictions between Indians and whites in Black Kettle's region, he continued to keep his own band at peace. On November 27, 1868, while camped along the banks of the Washita River in present-day Oklahoma, Black Kettle's band was once again attacked by soldiers. This time, however, the man of peace would not survive. He and about a hundred of his fellow Cheyenne died at the hands of the U.S. Seventh Cavalry, commanded that day by General George Armstrong Custer.

Today, the descendants of the Indians at Sand Creek Massacre are seeking restitution for the massacre from the United States government.

Geronimo

Apache patriot and resistance leader
1829?–1909

His name has become a war cry, a symbol of supreme courage and determination to defend a nation. Geronimo was the last and the best known of the Apache freedom fighters who resisted the intrusion of whites in the Southwest. For a quarter century the two cultures clashed violently. To the Apaches, Geronimo embodied the true Apache values, unyielding aggressiveness in war and deep attachment to his native land. But these very qualities inspired panic and hatred among settlers, who saw him as perhaps their fiercest enemy among all Indians.

The Apache tribes were a group of loosely organized peoples, with no overall leadership, who lived in bands or small groups of several extended families. Geronimo's group was part of a division of the Apaches called the Chiricahuas. The Chiricahuas inhabited rugged, dry lands in southern Arizona and New Mexico. Their way of life was mostly migratory, combining hunting, gathering wild plants, and some farming.

When food was scarce, which was frequently, the Chiricahua turned to raiding their neighbors. Raids and vengeance warfare were an honorable and expected part of Chiricahua life. By the time that American settlers began moving into their region, the Chiricahuas had already been through several centuries of warfare with the Spanish conquerors of Mexico, then the Mexicans, who had come to their territory looking for Indian slaves and Christian converts.

But during the 1860s and 1870s, group after group of Apaches was forced to submit to growing numbers of soldiers and settlers in their homeland. The U.S. army moved thousands of Apaches to the San Carlos Reservation, a barren stretch of land in central Arizona where they were told to become hard-working farmers.

The Chiricahuas, always tough and ingenious, were among the last of the Apache resisters. In their mountain strongholds, the scattered bands of resisters were led by a middle-aged warrior named Goyathlay. Non-Indians could not pronounce his real name, and he became known in Spanish as Geronimo. Geronimo's leadership was based on the great skill and determination he had exhibited in many battles. He was spurred on by a deep bitterness caused by the death of his family at the hands of Mexicans in 1858.

In 1876, the U.S. army tried to move the Chiricahuas to the San Carlos Reservation. Some gave up and went peacefully, but Geronimo and a band of followers who wanted no part of farming fled south into Mexico. For the next ten years, pursued intensively by the U.S. army, Geronimo alternately surrendered to reservation life in the United States and bolted to mountain hideouts where his band lived by raiding and plundering. For these fugitives it was a decade of desperation, defiance, and repeated betrayals and blunders by the U.S. army. For settlers in the region, it was a time of terror. Sensationalized press reports grossly exaggerated Geronimo's activities, making him the most infamous and hated of the Apaches.

In May 1885, Geronimo fled from San Carlos with several dozen warriors and their families. Army troops set out to capture him. The next March in Mexico, Geronimo gave himself up. But two days later, convinced that his captors were about to kill him, he and thirty-eight other Chiricahuas escaped.

Over the summer of 1886, he was hunted down again. His people grew very hungry and ragged, and their will to resist broke. The last few months of the campaign to bring in Geronimo required more than 5,000 soldiers and 500 scouts to track him and the remnants of his little band across 1,645 miles of desert. The army promised that after a period of exile, he could return to Arizona, so Geronimo finally surrendered in September.

Geronimo was now a prisoner of war. The army wanted to be sure that their long-time opponent would not be able to run away again. He and several hundred other Apaches, including peaceful Chiricahuas from San Carlos and even some scouts who had helped find Geronimo, were put on trains and sent into exile.

They were shipped first to St. Augustine, Florida, then to a camp in Alabama. About a quarter of them died of malaria or tuberculosis. Later many of the surviving Apaches were allowed to return to their home territory. But not Geronimo and his followers: they were allowed to join their traditional enemies, the Comanches and Kiowas, on a reservation in Oklahoma. Geronimo never again saw his native lands in Arizona.

Geronimo astride his horse (second from the left) in a picture from 1886 with fellow Apaches

In his later years, Geronimo learned to adjust to the expectations the white world had of him. He took up farming. He found a way to make money from his status as a legendary fighter. Under guard at fairs and expositions, he made public appearances, and he sold handcrafts and autographed pictures of himself. In 1905, he rode in the inaugural parade for President Theodore Roosevelt.

Geronimo repeatedly petitioned for a chance to visit his home but was refused. He died of pneumonia, still a prisoner of war, twenty-three years after his surrender. Four years later, in 1913, the last Chiricahuas were released and allowed to go home.

۶ა ۶ა ۶ა ۶ა

Sitting Bull

Hunkpapa Lakota tribal and spiritual leader

*c.*1831–1890

He wanted a vision of what lay ahead for his people, so he took part in the Sun Dance, the most sacred ceremony of the Plains Indians. As light filled the summer morning, he began his prayer song. He did not flinch when his adoptive brother cut fifty tiny pieces of flesh from each arm. He continued dancing without nourishment or rest for many hours, through the night, into the next day. Then he collapsed. At this time he had a vision of a battle in which his people were victorious. Sitting Bull's participation in the Sun Dance came at a critical time in the Lakota's resistance to white interference.

A few weeks later, on June 25, 1876, General George Armstrong Custer and a regiment of the U.S. Seventh Cavalry attacked the seven bands of the Lakota Nation and several families of Cheyenne and Arapaho following their annual Sun Dance. As a result of the attack, which was in violation of U.S. treaty agreements, several Indian warriors and every white soldier died that day. The Indians were victorious, just as Sitting Bull's vision had foretold.

Sitting Bull was a man of many abilities: a powerful chief, a spiritual man, and a shrewd politician and negotiator. Above all, he was devoted to his people —the Hunkpapa Lakota—and other bands of the Teton Lakota. He wanted to preserve their freedom to live unrestricted by white intruders in their traditional domain.

The Hunkpapas, one of the bands of the Teton Lakota/Dakota Nation, were known as great warriors, philosophers, and proud hunters. Their territory included what is now North Dakota, South Dakota, Minnesota, and parts of Wyoming and Montana. Early in his life, Sitting Bull showed he would excel as a hunter and warrior. He killed his first buffalo at ten, and he first "counted coup" (touched an enemy in battle) at fourteen. That same year, he completed his first vision quest. In his mid-twenties, he became leader of the Strong Heart warrior society, a prestigious group among the Lakota. This added to his recognition as a spiritual man and a wise and influential leader.

During the 1850s, the Lakota and Dakota began to feel the pressure of white expansion into the West. But Sitting Bull did not participate in conflicts with white pioneers until 1863, when the settlers' invasion of Hunkpapa hunting grounds directly threatened their existence. It was then that Sitting Bull became determined to resist white domination. In the next five years, he and his allies had many battles and skirmishes with the U.S. army.

For his leadership in these times, he was named principal chief of the entire Teton nation in 1867. When the war ended with the Fort Laramie Treaty of 1868, he did not accept the terms of the agreement, which put many Indians on a large reservation in the western Dakotas. Instead, Sitting Bull returned to open country, along with many other steadfast opponents of compromise.

After a few years of relative peace on the reservation, gold was discovered in the Black Hills in 1874. Even though these lands were sacred to the Lakota and Dakota and the treaties had guaranteed it would be theirs forever, gold prospectors with U.S. soldiers guarding them came flooding into the region. The angry Lakota, led by Sitting Bull, joined with Cheyennes and Arapahos to try to force the prospectors out. The Battle of the Little Bighorn on June 25, 1874, was their moment of greatest success. Following the Little Bighorn victory, Sitting Bull and his loyal followers headed for Canada.

By 1881, those of his group who were still with him were starving. Worn, but unbroken in spirit, Sitting Bull finally gave himself up to American army authorities. They held him prisoner for two years, then moved him to the Standing Rock Reservation in South Dakota. By then his exploits had made him a legendary figure across America. In 1885, tense authorities still saw him as a threat, a potential leader of a rebellion. Partly to get him off their hands, they released Sitting Bull. For a brief time, he joined the Buffalo Bill Wild West Show that toured throughout Europe.

Sitting Bull and Buffalo Bill Cody in a picture taken about 1880

Despite the various changes in Sitting Bull's life, many Lakota still regarded him as their chief and principal spokesman. When the U.S. government wanted to split up Indian lands by buying back large areas—at a very low price—Sitting Bull counseled other native leaders to resist the proposal. He vigorously protested against any attempt at all to break up Lakota lands. In the end, a few of Sitting Bull's rivals and some government-appointed chiefs found the revised offer too good to refuse. The reservation was broken up and parts sold with their names, but not his, on the agreement.

Jealousies and divisions steadily grew as many Lakota lost their traditional ways of life and settled on reservations. Eventually these tensions led to Sitting Bull's death. In 1890, some Lakota began to adopt the new Ghost Dance religion, a movement that promised its followers deliverance from white people. Sitting Bull permitted Ghost Dancing at his camp. Fearing Sitting Bull's influence might inspire an uprising, the Indian Bureau's agent ordered Sitting Bull's arrest and dispatched Indian police to bring him in. At daybreak on December 15, they stormed into his cabin and pulled him from bed. Hot words flew, drawing a crowd of Sitting Bull's supporters outside. Shooting started; when it was over, seven Indian police, eight Ghost Dancers, and Sitting Bull lay dead.

In his lifetime Sitting Bull exhibited a rare quality of leadership. He was and continues to be admired for his devout spirituality and his steadfast courage, strength, and determination to live according to his beliefs and the ways of his people.

ãô ãô ãô ãô

Chief Joseph
Nez Perce patriot, chief, and resistance leader
*c.*1840–1904

In the summer of 1877, the Pacific Northwest was the scene of a courageous, desperate journey by a band of Indian people. The people were normally peaceful, but they had become entangled in a war over their homelands. Although their dearest wish was simply to stay on the lands that they had long regarded as home, they were forced to flee. Their principal leader was a chief whose extraordinary dignity and devotion to duty brought him sympathy and renown even during the journey that brought his people's hopes to a sad end.

His name was In-mut-too-yah-lat-lat ("Thunder coming up over the land from the water"), but he became famous as Chief Joseph. His people were the Nez Perce, a group native to western Idaho and the adjoining areas of Oregon and Washington. They were traditionally game hunters and salmon fishers, but in the 1700s some Nez Perce began to breed and trade horses. By the 1800s, they had developed huge herds. The Appaloosa horse, a sturdy, handsomely spotted breed, was their specialty.

For a long time, the Nez Perce had friendly and productive relations with white people. Soon after the Lewis and Clark expedition visited their region in 1805, trappers and fur traders arrived and established trading relations. Not long after that, Christian missionaries arrived. Among the Indians who converted to Christianity was Joseph's father, Old Joseph. Joseph spent much of his childhood at a mission community. By the 1840s, however, many homesteaders were arriving and claiming Nez Perce lands for their own. Friendly relations between Indians and non-Indians deteriorated as the settlers took more and more land away from the Indians.

Old Joseph was leader of a major Nez Perce band whose ancestral home was the green and fertile Wallowa valley of Oregon. In 1855, Old Joseph and most other Nez Perce leaders agreed to a treaty with the U.S. government that let their people retain much of their traditional lands, including the Wallowa valley. A few years later, however, gold was discovered in the region, and newcomers arrived to take it. In 1863, U.S. government officials negotiated a new treaty with the Nez Perce that drastically reduced the extent of their land. Some Nez Perce leaders accepted the new treaty, but not Old Joseph, for it would have meant losing the Wallowa valley and moving to Idaho. In the following years, the "nontreaty" Nez Perce made no open quarrel with the whites, but they firmly resisted all government efforts to keep them away from their traditional hunting grounds.

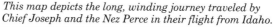

This map depicts the long, winding journey traveled by Chief Joseph and the Nez Perce in their flight from Idaho.

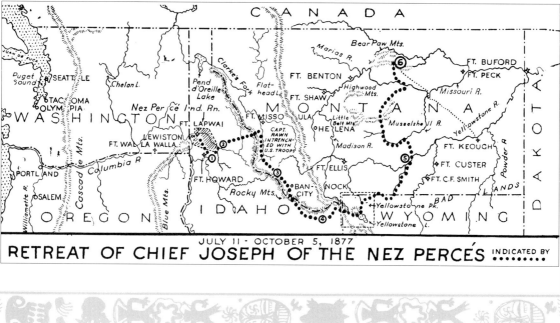

70

In 1871, when Old Joseph died, his son Joseph became the principal civil chief, or peace chief, of the band. Despite growing pressures from settlers and government officials, he and the other nontreaty leaders continued to peacefully resist relocation.

The showdown came in 1877. That spring the U.S. government was preparing to force the Indians out of the Wallowa valley and onto the Idaho reservation. A few young Nez Perce men got into a fight with white settlers and killed them.

Chief Joseph urged calm. But when army troops came to round up dissenters, some Nez Perce fought them off. After several more skirmishes, the Indian leaders reluctantly decided that all hope of living peacefully in the Wallowa valley was gone. They were at war, they were vastly outnumbered, and their only reasonable alternative was to retreat to Montana buffalo country.

For the next four months, the Nez Perce were pursued by General O. O. Howard and the U.S. army over 1,500 miles of rugged terrain, winding through the mountains of Idaho, Wyoming, and Montana. They were mostly women, children, and old men, and they were hampered by having to take all their possessions with them. Only about one hundred and fifty of the roughly five hundred and fifty Indians were warriors, although many of these were highly experienced, skillful fighters. Guided by Joseph and several war chiefs, the Nez Perce outwitted, outmaneuvered, and outfought a force of 5,000 army troops.

As the summer wore on, newspaper accounts documented the Nez Perce plight and Chief Joseph's leadership. Because Joseph had often been the tribe's spokesman, the army assumed that he was their commander, and he acquired a reputation as a military genius. Even to his opponents, Joseph seemed honest, decent, and interested in minimizing violence toward civilians. People also admired the fact that between battles, the Nez Perce peacefully traded for supplies at white settlements, without complaining about the high prices some whites demanded.

The months of fighting and forced marches through rugged country were an increasing strain on the Nez Perce. As more people were wounded or fell sick, travel became still more difficult. Yet the U.S. army kept pursuing the weary Indians. Hoping to escape into Canada, the Nez Perce turned north. By the end of September, however, exhaustion, bad weather, and lack of food stopped them. In northern Montana, just thirty miles from the Canadian border, they were attacked by fresh military forces. The siege lasted for five days. Finally, on October 5, Joseph surrendered. The Nez Perce were divided about surrendering. Indians who were unwilling to surrender had stolen away during the night. Some reached Canada; others were caught later.

During the parley for surrender, an army officer recorded Joseph's speech to his headmen and the scouts who had been sent by Howard. Although there are slightly different versions of this speech, each confirms Joseph's heroic stand on behalf of his people.

> Tell General Howard I know his heart. What he told me before I have in my heart. I am tired of fighting. Our chiefs are killed. Looking Glass is dead. Too-hul-hul-sote is dead. The old men are all dead. It is the young men who say yes or no. He who led on the young men is dead. It is cold and we have no blankets. The little children are freezing to death. My people, some of them, have run away to the hills, and have no blankets, no food; no one knows where they are—perhaps freezing to death. I want to have time to look for my children and see how many of them I can find. Maybe I shall find them among the dead. Hear me, my chiefs. I am tired; my heart is sick and sad. From where the sun now stands I will fight no more forever.

Chief Joseph and his followers were solemnly promised that they would be sent to the same reservation in Idaho that they had sought to avoid by fleeing a few months earlier. Instead, they were sent to Kansas and later to the humid lowlands of Indian Territory (now the state of Oklahoma), where they were told to become farmers. Many died there of malaria and starvation.

Chief Joseph tried every possible appeal to federal authorities to return the Nez Perce to the lands where their ancestors were buried. He traveled twice to Washington, D.C., to present their pleas. In 1885, Joseph and most of his band were sent to a reservation in Washington state—a place very different from his beloved Wallowa valley. Still in exile there nineteen years later, Joseph died—of a broken heart, the reservation doctor reported.

Crazy Horse
Lakota war chief
*c.*1841–1877

He always rode into battle dressed as the warrior he saw in his vision, with a stone behind one ear, his long hair unbraided and flying, his cheek painted with a lightning streak, and his body painted with hailstone dots. Crazy Horse was young, quiet, and thoughtful. To many of his people, he embodied their best and noblest hope. He was one of the courageous warriors of the proud, strong Lakota nation, who, in the 1860s and 1870s, defended their families and land from invasion. With fierce tenacity, the warriors resisted white expansion into their territory. Crazy Horse, who fearlessly fought to defend his people's freedom, was one of their most brilliant and determined military leaders.

Crazy Horse was born just to the east of the Black Hills, in what is now South Dakota. His father was a medicine man (a spiritual man and healer) of the Oglala band of the Teton Lakota/Dakota nation. His mother was the daughter of a chief of the Brule band of the Lakota. Little is known of his childhood other than that when he was young, people remarked on his curly hair, pale skin, mild manner, and mystical ways. But before he was twelve he passed a difficult rite of passage on the path to becoming a warrior when he killed his first buffalo and received his own horse.

About the same time, Crazy Horse witnessed U.S. army attacks on the Lakota. Like all boys in their teens, he underwent the vision quest that changed his life. Crazy Horse fasted for four days and nights crying for a vision that would give him guidance in life. Through the vision that Crazy Horse was given, he was guided toward a life of austerity and bravery. By the time he was seventeen, he had achieved full warrior status, riding in a raid on the Crow Indians.

In 1864, violence flared in Indian country when whites attacked the Cheyenne and Arapaho at Sand Creek, Colorado. After the Sand Creek Massacre, the Oglalas, Crazy Horse among them, were drawn into warfare with the U.S. army and settlers and miners moving into Indian lands.

Over the next several years, it became clear that Crazy Horse was a great leader. He joined with Red Cloud, the war chief who led the Lakotas in a drive to close down the Bozeman Trail, which was the route to recently opened gold fields in Montana. Again and again in raids that he led, Crazy Horse showed his boldness as an individual fighter and his skill as a military planner and commander of other warriors. Eventually the U.S. government gave in to Lakota pressure, agreeing to abandon military forts along the Bozeman Trail if the raids were stopped. But in 1868 Red Cloud, along with other leaders, signed the Treaty of Fort Laramie, which would force the Lakota to live on a reservation. Unwilling to live on a reservation, Crazy Horse, along with many other Indians, moved to open country to continue their traditional way of life.

Their freedom was not to last. Survey crews, in violation of an 1868 treaty, began to make plans to cut a railroad across Indian territory. When Crazy Horse led raids against the surveyors, the U.S. army sent protection in the form of Seventh Cavalry forces, commanded by George Armstrong Custer. Then in 1874, gold was discovered in the Black Hills on lands that according to treaties belonged to Indians. Nonetheless, white prospectors, protected by the army, rushed to the region, provoking further hostilities. In late 1875, authorities in Washington ordered another military campaign to subdue all Indians and move them to reservations. Crazy Horse played a leading role in the Indian resistance to this order, culminating in June 1876 with the spectacular victory of the Lakota, Cheyenne, and Arapaho at the Battle of the Little Bighorn, often called Custer's Last Stand.

This battle was the last great success for the Lakota. Determined to defeat the Indians, the army pursued them with a vengeance. Crazy Horse led his warriors back to the hills, but the following winter was bitterly cold, game was scarce, and the U.S. government was offering supplies to all Indians who came to the reservation voluntarily. In May 1877, Crazy Horse and about a thousand resisters finally gave up their fight at the Red Cloud Agency in Nebraska. As they approached Fort Robinson near the agency, they began to sing war songs. One officer is reported to have remarked, "This is a triumphal march, not a surrender!"

The funeral procession for Chief Crazy Horse

There is no evidence to suggest that Crazy Horse was planning to mount a new rebellion, but military authorities suspected that the Indians who had resisted them so well would sooner or later resist again. Although Crazy Horse was confined to reservation land, within a few months the authorities decided it would be best to arrest him. Eight companies of cavalry and four hundred Indians led by Red Cloud were sent to bring him in. Crazy Horse cooperated until he realized he was about to be imprisoned. Then he suddenly pulled a knife out of his blanket, and a guard stabbed him with a bayonet.

Crazy Horse died the next day. His father and stepmother removed his body to an unknown place. Legend has it that this honored patriot of the Lakota nation was buried near Wounded Knee Creek, in South Dakota, the site of the famous massacre thirteen years later.

Sarah Winnemucca
Paiute activist, scout, interpreter, teacher, and writer
*c.*1844–1891

Sarah Winnemucca was a tireless advocate for the rights of her people, the Northern Paiute, in a time when they faced devastation and drastic change. Many of her efforts on behalf of the Paiutes eventually failed. Yet her valor and energy, and the size of the task she attempted, made her one of the most famous Indian women of the 1800s.

For centuries the Paiute people led an undisturbed life of hunting and food-gathering on the desert plateau of western Nevada. But a few years after Sarah was born, settlers began moving into the region. Increasingly, they came into conflict with the Paiutes. Sarah's grandfather Truckee, who had been a guide to earlier white explorers, encouraged cooperation and friendship with the newcomers. When Sarah was six, Truckee took some of his family, including Sarah, on an extended visit to work on a ranch in California. It was her first chance to observe non-Indian people's ways and to begin learning their languages, Spanish and English.

Sarah continued to live in both the white and the Paiute worlds. When she was about thirteen, Sarah lived for a year with a white stagecoach agent's family in Nevada. She was employed to do housework and be a companion to their daughter. Always quick to learn, Sarah became very good at speaking English. She also learned some reading and writing. Later she briefly attended a convent school in California, which she had to leave because some parents of white students objected to an Indian being educated with their daughters. Thus, by her middle teens, she knew not only the ancient Paiute customs, but also much of how white people lived and thought.

In 1859, silver was discovered in Paiute territory and a steady stream of miners began appearing. The following year tensions erupted into a series of conflicts now called the Paiute War. The war and the continuing clashes between Indians and non-Indians disrupted life and caused terrible suffering for the Paiutes. Sarah lost a number of relatives, including a baby brother. Nonetheless, in an attempt to minimize the bloodshed, she sometimes acted as a peacemaker between whites and Indians. Often her efforts were met with suspicion or outright opposition from one side or the other.

When the war was over, the United States controlled the region. American soldiers were posted at forts in the area, and the Paiutes were put onto a newly established reservation near Reno, Nevada. On the reservation, the Paiutes' welfare was in the hands of Indian Bureau agents, who represented the U.S. government. Some agents were generous, decent men who did their best with limited resources, but too many were corrupt. The worst agents did not hesitate to steal supplies meant for the Indians, causing many Paiutes to suffer and even die. Sarah grew to hate the agents who mistreated her people, and she began to protest. In 1870, she traveled to San Francisco to tell the authorities about the agents' wrong doings. She received some publicity, but no real help.

Sarah had more faith in the U.S. military than the Indian Bureau agents. She knew and trusted certain army officers. She became convinced that her people would be treated more fairly if the soldiers at the forts managed the reservation supplies instead of the dishonest agents. Many starving Paiutes already flocked to the forts to receive rations, rather than endure grim reservation conditions.

Because of her knowledge of English, Spanish, and three Indian languages, Sarah was hired as an interpreter at Camp McDermit, in northern Nevada. When in 1872, the Paiutes were moved to a new reservation in Oregon, Sarah accompanied them as an interpreter; later she also taught in a school there.

*A gathering of Bannock, the people who held
Sarah Winnemucca's father and others captive in 1878*

In 1878, at the start of the Bannock War in Oregon and Idaho, Sarah's father and several other Paiutes were held captive by Bannock Indians. No one, neither army soldier nor Paiute, appeared willing to risk bringing them out of Bannock territory. So Sarah volunteered to serve as a scout to find the captives. The mission was dangerous and exhausting, but Sarah found her father's group and returned them to safety. When the Bannock War ended, the Paiutes were ordered to go to yet another reservation, this one in Washington state. Sarah was very distressed by the move, which uprooted her people once again and forced them to undertake a cruel journey in winter.

The next year Sarah traveled again to San Francisco, this time to deliver her first public lecture. She made an emotion-filled appeal for Indian rights and told how Indian agents had mistreated the Paiutes. She began to awaken the interest and sympathy of the public, but some newspapers spread slanderous lies about her character. Sarah kept up her efforts despite the false charges. She next visited Washington, D.C., where she met with President Rutherford B. Hayes and the Interior Secretary, Carl Schurz. They agreed to help the Paiutes, but the improvements they promised never happened.

In 1881, Sarah married Lambert Hopkins, a U.S. army lieutenant. With his encouragement, she set out on another speaking tour in the East. Again her aim was to publicize the plight of Indians and encourage changes in government policy. This time several influential people took up her cause. She reached more than three hundred audiences and was able to gather thousands of signatures for a petition. To raise money for the trip, she wrote a vividly detailed and successful book, *Life Among the Paiutes, Their Wrongs and Claims*. But government decision-makers steered a different course than she hoped, and Paiute hopes for justice were dashed once more.

Worn out by her struggles to help her people, Sarah's health began to weaken. She gave up public speaking and went back to teaching school for several years in the 1880s. After her husband died, she retired to live at her sister's house in Montana, where she died at the age of forty-seven.

ॐ ॐ ॐ ॐ

The La Flesche Family

Susette La Flesche
Ponca and Omaha Indian rights worker
1854–1903

Francis La Flesche
Ponca and Omaha anthropologist and writer
1857–1932

Susan La Flesche
Ponca and Omaha physician
1865–1915

Their father, Iron Eye, or Joseph La Flesche, once wrote to a member of his family: "Look ahead and you will see nothing but the white man. The future is full of the white man, and we shall be as nothing before them." La Flesche, of mixed Ponca and French ancestry, realized that Indian people faced many rapid and difficult changes. He felt the best way to prepare his children for the future was to raise them to survive in the white world, but be proud of their Indian heritage.

The La Flesche family lived on the Omaha reservation in what is now Nebraska. Joseph was a prosperous merchant and an important leader in his community. He was appointed chief of the Omahas, despite having no hereditary claim to the position. In accordance with Omaha custom, Joseph had several wives. Francis, Joseph's son, had a different mother from Susette and Susan.

Susette became the most famous of her family. As a lecturer and writer, she brought national attention to unjust laws and policies affecting Native Americans. Like her younger brother and sister, she began her schooling at a Presbyterian mission school on the reservation. Later, she attended the Elizabeth Institute for Young Ladies, in New Jersey, where she adopted some of the customs of middle-class whites.

Pictured above: Susette La Flesche

Susette rocketed to fame because of a case concerning U.S. government treatment of the Poncas, a tribe closely related to the Omahas. In 1877, the Poncas were forcibly moved from their lands in Nebraska to Indian Territory (now the state of Oklahoma). Many Poncas died of disease and hardship during the next two years. Their chief, Standing Bear, tried to lead a band of followers back home, but the group was captured, and Standing Bear was arrested.

The plight of the Poncas and Standing Bear was widely publicized, especially by Thomas Tibbles, a newspaperman with the *Omaha Herald*. Susette and other Ponca supporters rallied support for the prisoners until they were eventually released. Tibbles, Standing Bear, Susette, and Francis La Flesche went on a lecture tour of the eastern states to publicize further the unfairness of the government's treatment of Indians. It was on this tour that Susette grew into the role of committed reformer.

As a speaker, Susette was forceful and eloquent, and she was not afraid to use her Omaha identity in presenting her point. On tour, she went by her Indian name, Inshtatheumba (which means Bright Eyes) and wore native clothing in public appearances. Audiences found Susette a fascinating, impressive speaker for her cause. Her educational background had prepared her to mingle easily with the famous and well-to-do. Upon meeting her, a group of prominent Bostonians was moved to form an organization that was influential in the passage of the Dawes Act of 1887.

In 1881, Susette married Thomas Tibbles. The two continued to lecture on Indian rights in the United States and in Europe. Susette also developed as a writer and artist. She edited Standing Bear's story, *Ploughed Under: The Story of an Indian Chief*; wrote articles for newspapers and magazines; and illustrated a book. Susette La Flesche signed her work "Bright Eyes."

Susan La Flesche, Susette's younger sister, also became a reformer, but of a different kind. She was the first Indian woman physician and spent much of her life working to improve the health of her people.

Susan attended the Elizabeth Institute like her sister, then the Hampton Institute in Virginia, one of the first off-reservation government schools for Indians. Her academic excellence led to a scholarship to the Women's Medical College of Pennsylvania, in Philadelphia, where in 1889 she graduated at the top of her class.

Susan returned to the reservation in Nebraska. Soon she was in charge of the health care of all the Omahas. She worked tirelessly, traveling many miles on horseback in all kinds of weather to see her patients. She took an interest in improving living conditions for the Omahas and in teaching health practices

Susan La Flesche

Francis La Flesche

that would avoid the spread of disease. For example, she campaigned against the use of public drinking cups. Horrified by the destructive effects of alcohol abuse, she worked vigorously against the distribution of liquor among the Omaha. She was very interested in the Christian religion, and she served as a medical missionary to her people. Her activities earned her the deep admiration and appreciation of all who knew her.

In 1894, Susan married Henri Picotte, who was French and Sioux, and they had two sons. The strain of her work took a toll on her health, and she was frequently ill during her career.

Francis La Flesche, called Frank, was a half-brother to Susette and Susan. He too was a champion of Indian rights, and he became a scholar, writer, lawyer, and a respected authority on Indian cultures. More than his sisters, he liked to return periodically to participate in the traditional life of the Omaha.

Although Frank attended the reservation mission school, he also learned much about traditional Omaha culture when he was young. He took part in tribal ceremonials and in some of the last buffalo hunts on the Great Plains. He later described his boyhood in *The Middle Five*, a memoir that is still considered an outstanding account of a youth in two cultures.

For many years Frank worked with the noted anthropologist Alice Fletcher, researching Omaha life. From 1881 to 1910, he was an interpreter and advisor at the Bureau of Indian Affairs in Washington, D.C. During this period, he also obtained a law degree. In 1910, he took another research post as an anthropologist, and from then until the end of his life, he worked on studies of the Osage people and language.

Judging by the accomplishments of Iron Eye's children, his plan for them worked well indeed. The La Flesches managed in their different ways to merge the Indian and non-Indian worlds, and they never lost sight of their primary goal of improving the quality of life for Indian people.

❧ ❧ ❧ ❧

Charles Alexander Eastman

Santee Dakota physician and writer
1858–1939

The newly appointed young doctor from the Indian agency frantically searched for survivors among the frozen heaps of bodies. Three days before, on this snowy sunlit field near Wounded Knee Creek, more than two hundred Lakota had been killed or wounded by the U.S. Seventh Cavalry. Dr. Charles Eastman, whose experiences included both a traditional Santee Dakota upbringing and an elite education in the white world, felt shock and outrage. He had based his entire adult life on his conviction that American Indians would have to learn to live in the white world if they were to survive at all. Yet this tragic scene showed him, perhaps for the first time, that being an Indian involved in the white world could mean profound suffering.

Until he was fifteen, Charles Eastman lived a life almost entirely separated from the white world. He was born on the Santee Dakota reservation in Redwood Falls, Minnesota. His early name was Hakadah, "The Last One," because his mother died shortly after his birth; several years later he received another name, Ohiyesa, "The Victor." His father was imprisoned and believed dead after the 1862 conflict between white settlers and Santee Dakota called the Minnesota Uprising. After this tragedy, Ohiyesa was taken to Canada and raised there by his grandmother and uncle. He was taught to be a woodland hunter and warrior in the ancient traditional way of his Dakota ancestors.

In 1872, Ohiyesa's father, now a Christian convert, suddenly reappeared in the boy's life and took him to Flandreau, South Dakota, to attend a mission school. Baptized as Charles Eastman, the young man began a seventeen-year educational adventure that immersed him in the Christian religion. He grew to feel that the old Indian world was forever changed, and that Indians must adjust to a new life within white society. Through education, he could learn how best to help his people adapt, and also serve as a guidepost for others to follow.

After two years at Flandreau, Eastman transferred to a school in Nebraska—and walked the entire 150 miles to get there. Later he attended Dartmouth College in New Hampshire where he graduated with a bachelor's degree in 1887, and Boston University, where he earned a medical doctor's degree in 1890. He was one of the first Indians ever to receive an M.D.

It was only a month after he took his first job, at Pine Ridge Agency in South Dakota, that Eastman saw the victims at Wounded Knee. Deeply disturbed, he became more determined to work to improve the lives of Indians. His medical career with the Indian Bureau, however, was soon troubled by disputes with other officials. Within a few years he resigned to pursue other service activities on behalf of Indian people.

At Pine Ridge, Eastman met Elaine Goodale, a white teacher and writer from Massachusetts who shared many of his ideals. They were married in 1891 and raised six children before they separated thirty years later. Elaine helped Charles with his writing career, which would eventually produce nine books and many magazine articles. Using a pencil and scratch paper, Charles would produce a draft, which Elaine typed and revised.

Juggling his writing with a variety of other jobs, Eastman became one of the most prominent Indian leaders of his day. For the most part, he did not practice medicine. He worked for the Young Men's Christian Association, heading a program that eventually established more than forty Indian YMCAs around the United States. He acted as an advocate for the Santee Dakota in Washington, D.C., presenting their claims before government bodies.

Between 1903 and 1909, Eastman was involved in a federal project to rename all the Dakota and Lakota. Under the 1887 General Allotment Act,

During his lifetime, Charles Eastman established more than forty YMCAs for Indians.
Here is the White Clay YMCA at Pine Ridge Reservation in South Dakota.

individual Indians and their heirs were to have legal title to own land. Traditional Dakota/Lakota naming customs, however, made it difficult to keep track of people and avoid property conflicts. Eastman believed that rightfully owning the land they lived on could only help his people. So he agreed to help clarify family relationships and revise traditional Indian names.

Eastman focused many of his energies on helping young people. He helped found the Boy Scouts of America and with his family established and operated a summer children's camp in New Hampshire. He was also active in Indian organizations and reform movements and served as president of the intertribal Society of American Indians.

But Charles Eastman became best known as a writer and lecturer on Indian culture and history. He wrote two autobiographies: *Indian Boyhood* (1902), the story of the first fifteen years of his life; and *From the Deep Woods to Civilization* (1916), about his adult experiences and his criticisms of government Indian policy. Other books and articles described Lakota/Dakota religion and customs and his views on relations between Indians and whites. In all his works Eastman tried to promote understanding of Indians and influence his white readers to support the cause of reform. The popularity of his writings led to many lecture engagements across the United States and in England in which he spoke on the same themes.

Throughout Charles Eastman's long and varied career he never encouraged Indians to abandon their traditional cultures. Rather, he argued, they should remember and value their Indian heritage but set aside many of its practices. For himself, he comfortably accepted that he was always clearly an Indian, although he had adopted the outward forms of the white world. Yet he also felt the pressures of living in a white society that didn't always measure up to its promises, and of being a symbol of successful cultural blending. In his last years, he built a cabin on an island in Lake Huron, near his Canadian boyhood home.

ﻪ‌ ﻪ‌ ﻪ‌ ﻪ‌

Wovoka

Northern Paiute religious leader
1858?–1932

His message offered bright hope in a time of dark despair: if the Indian people lived properly and practiced the correct rituals, their dead kin would be resurrected to join them in a peaceful life on a bountiful land, and the whites would all go away. A mystic and a visionary, Wovoka preached a renewal of the traditional American Indian world through the Ghost Dance religion. At a time when the Plains tribes were being systematically killed or forced to live in increasingly wretched conditions, his message had a profound, if brief, impact on many of them.

Wovoka was a Northern Paiute from the desert of western Nevada. He grew up steeped in Paiute spiritual beliefs. His father, Tavibo, was a medicine man who had been part of an earlier Ghost Dance movement.

When Wovoka was in his early teens, Tavibo died. The orphaned Wovoka went to live and work as a farmhand on a nearby ranch owned by a white family named Wilson. They called him Jack, and he became known among whites as Jack Wilson. The Wilsons were devout, Bible-reading Presbyterians, and hoping to develop him spiritually, they encouraged Jack to learn about Christianity.

For about ten years, Wovoka was an ordinary, obscure, hard-working man. Then he returned to live again among the Paiute and developed a reputation as a prophet and a medicine man. In late 1888, Wovoka fell ill and developed a high fever. On January 1, 1889, during a solar eclipse, while he was ill, he had a trancelike experience. When he recovered, Wovoka reported that during his trance he had visited the Supreme Being. He had been promised that one day soon the Indian world would be joyously transformed, as long as people followed certain simple rules.

To achieve the promised state of happiness, the Paiute would have to live peacefully, be honest and decent in all their actions, clean themselves often, and never use alcohol. Many of these ideas were similar to the Christian teachings that Wovoka had encountered while living with the Wilsons.

The new creed recalled the Ghost Dance movement from Tavibo's time. Wovoka said Indians should perform the Ghost Dance, a round dance where participants joined hands and circled slowly to the left in time to the chant of songs Wovoka had learned in his vision. In addition, they should keep to their native ways of life, avoiding customs of the whites. If the Paiute kept to these practices, game animals would return, dead friends would live again, and white people and all the suffering they caused would disappear. Life would be as if they were in paradise.

Soon Wovoka had other trancelike experiences and brought back more and more messages from the Supreme Being. Some of them were unclear or contradictory. Although Indian people eagerly welcomed the hope he offered for their future, Wovoka's followers interpreted his visions in different ways. Some began to consider him the prophet of a new religion; others even worshiped him as a messiah. So the Ghost Dance religion's doctrine was not understood the same way everywhere it spread. And it spread rapidly, especially among the peoples of Great Plains, who were half-starved and increasingly hemmed in by soldiers and homesteaders.

Especially among one Plains group, the Lakota, people began to believe that if they wore "ghost shirts," white garments decorated with special emblems, enemy bullets could not harm them. By the summer of 1890, their Ghost Dance fervor began to alarm nearby settlers. The nervous white people asked them-selves, why would an Indian want protection from bullets unless he was planning a fight?

Tensions and misunderstandings between whites and Lakota reached a terrible climax in December 1890, at Wounded Knee, South Dakota. Contemporary published accounts reported that about two hundred Lakota men, women, and children were slaughtered by troops of the army's Seventh Cavalry regiment. Oral accounts suggest as many as 426 dead. Among the dead were many who wore ghost shirts. When Wovoka learned what happened at

The Sun Dance

happened at Wounded Knee, he was very distressed. His messages had been about peace and deliverance, not bloodshed. Wovoka went into hiding.

The following spring, many of Ghost Dance faithful hoped the world would be transformed, but the grinding hardships did not disappear from their lives. Their ghost shirts had failed, and the great change had not come. Many saddened believers lost their faith. The Ghost Dance religion was collapsing.

Wovoka finally reappeared to renew his teachings. He condemned the misinterpretations of his ideas, such as belief in the power of ghost shirts. He continued to predict a worldly transformation and to advocate a return to the old Indian life. For many years, there were still people who believed in him and his vision.

Wounded Knee

Wounded Knee is a name with powerful symbolic meaning. On maps, Wounded Knee is both a creek and a nearby small village. In the hearts of many Americans, both Indian and non-Indian, the name Wounded Knee recalls a painful injustice from the past.

On December 29, 1890, in a field just west of Wounded Knee Creek on the Pine Ridge Reservation in southwestern South Dakota, a massacre took place. In effect, this massacre brought an end to the Indian wars of resistance against white expansion across North America. By the 1880s, settlers had overrun nearly all of the territory that Indians traditionally had called home. The effect of this was to undermine or destroy the ancient ways of life for many native peoples. Torn from their cultural roots, Indians were forced to adjust to the confinement of reservations, where living conditions were abysmal. People were poorly fed and housed, sick, ignored or mistreated by officials. At Pine Ridge, the stresses faced by the Lakota provoked an explosive situation.

Big Foot's band gathering in August 1890. A few months later most of the men pictured were killed by the U.S. Seventh Cavalry at Wounded Knee Creek.

For years before the massacre, the Lakota had searched for an answer to their miseries. Many had recently accepted the new Ghost Dance religion preached by the Northern Paiute prophet Wovoka. Among the promises made to believers in that religion was that white people would soon disappear from the earth and the buffalo would become plentiful again. Reservation officials feared that the Lakota were about to start an armed rebellion. When Sitting Bull seemed to encourage the Ghost Dance, the authorities moved to arrest him, and in the process, killed him and a number of his followers on December 15, 1890.

Some of Sitting Bull's followers fled, hoping to find safety. They joined Big Foot's band, who were in the process of moving their camp to Pine Ridge. Remnants of the Seventh Cavalry, who were sent to intercept Big Foot and his followers, found them late on December 28. Big Foot surrendered peacefully, and prisoners and soldiers camped overnight by Wounded Knee Creek. The next morning, as soldiers were searching the camp for weapons, a shot was fired. Suddenly the encampment was a killing field. The soldiers, who surrounded the Indians, had rifles and machine guns, which they fired at close range at men, women, and children armed with little more than knives and clubs. Big Foot, who was sick with pneumonia, was shot in the head as he tried to rise from his bed. Accounts published at the time said about two hundred Indian men, women, and children were killed and many wounded; about thirty soldiers died, some of them accidentally shot by other soldiers in crossfire.

Indian bodies lay on the frozen ground for three days while a blizzard swept over them. On New Year's Day, 1891, a burial crew arrived to chip away the ice and bury the remains in a common grave. Newspaper reporters also came, and photographers took haunting pictures of the scene. The compelling images and descriptions that they provided made a deep impression on the public. The era of mass violence against American Indians was drawing to a close in the West, but this episode was the first where images of the ugly result were there for everyone to see. Unfortunately, most Americans focused on the sensational aspects of the incident, rather than the policies that led to such a slaughter.

*The frozen bodies of dead Lakota lay on the battlefield
for several days before being dumped into a common burial grave.*

Eight decades later, images and memories of 1890 still lingered in the hearts and minds of many American Indians. By 1973, much had changed at the Pine Ridge Reservation, but too much was the same. There, as on many Indian reservations across the country, poverty, government neglect, and lack of opportunity were chronic problems.

In 1973, the little town of Wounded Knee became the site of a major protest action by a militant activist organization, the American Indian Movement (AIM). AIM's purpose for the protest was to spotlight history and the ongoing plight of Indians. Controversy arose because of the way AIM attempted to achieve political goals related to Lakota tribal leadership at Pine Ridge.

On February 27, about two hundred AIM members took control of the village of Wounded Knee, declaring their intention to stay until several demands had been met. AIM leaders Russell Means and Dennis Banks demanded that Richard Wilson, the elected tribal chairman of the Oglala Sioux, be removed from office and the tribal government be replaced by a new one. They also wanted the U.S. Senate to investigate some 371 broken treaties with Indians and the mistreatment of Indians by the Bureau of Indian Affairs.

Federal law enforcement officers surrounded the town. Armed AIM members barricaded themselves in buildings. The situation became a siege that lasted until May 8. During the seventy-one-day takeover of the town, there were various negotiations and exchanges of gunfire. Two Indians were killed, and one federal marshal was seriously wounded. Eventually the confrontation ended when the occupiers of the town agreed to withdraw and the federal officials agreed to discuss AIM's charges and to investigate the tribal government.

The occupation of Wounded Knee was widely reported in the press, and the American public became a little more educated about Indian issues, thus partly achieving one of AIM's goals. But AIM's action also drew sharp criticism. Many elected tribal leaders across the country disagreed with AIM's philosophy and methods. Although surrounded by controvery, the siege at Wounded Knee gripped the attention of many Americans and breathed new life into old hopes for justice.

In 1986, Oglalas Alex White Plume and Birgil Kills Straight, with a group of nineteen riders, reenacted Big Foot's 150-mile journey to Wounded Knee on horseback. Each December, for the next four years, the group made the journey again. The final trip, led by Arval Looking Horse, Minneconjou, and Keeper of the Sacred Calf Pipe culminated in a ceremony called "The Wiping of Tears."

This journey marked the hundredth anniversary of the Wounded Knee Massacre. For the first time, survivors and their families could publicly mourn those who died at Wounded Knee and work through the grief that many may have been carrying for a very long time.

Ishi
The last Yahi
c.1862–1916

One August morning in 1911, a starving, exhausted, frightened man stumbled out of the hills of northern California into the town of Oroville and into the twentieth century. Ishi was the sole survivor of the Yahi, a fiercely independent native people who had been displaced and killed by whites for generations. Ishi expected that he too would be killed that day, but instead he began a second life.

Ishi's people, the Yahi, were probably never very numerous. They were one branch of a small tribal group called the Yana, but they had their own dialect and traditional territory. For thousands of years, the Yahi hunted, fished, and gathered edible and useful plants in the dry, rugged country above the valley of the Sacramento River into the Sierra Nevada mountains. Then in the middle of the 1800s, gold prospectors and other settlers began to drive the Yahi out of their native lands. Indians and non-Indians attacked and counterattacked each other, and by 1870 it seemed that all the Yahi were dead.

Unknown to the outside world, a handful of Yahi had escaped, including the child Ishi and his mother. Hoping to avoid the extinction of their tribe, they set out to completely conceal their existence from the whites. In 1908, however, the tiny band was accidentally discovered, and all but Ishi were killed.

Ishi managed to hide out alone in the wilderness for three more years. Finally, out of food and desperate, he walked into Oroville. The local authorities did not know what to do with this man who did not speak English. For lack of a better idea, they put Ishi in the town jail.

Within days, two anthropologists at the University of California, Thomas Waterman and Alfred Kroeber, read in the newspapers about the "wild man of Oroville." Guessing that Ishi might be a survivor of the presumably extinct Yahi, Waterman visited him at the jail. He was delighted when Ishi recognized some of the words from a Yana vocabulary list. Ishi, too, was delighted—for the first time in years, he was communicating with another human being. Excited and relieved to have someone to talk to, Ishi poured out his story, even though Waterman at that point understood only a small fraction of his words.

Waterman and Kroeber arranged for Ishi to live in San Francisco at the University's Museum of Anthropology, where Kroeber was the director. For his part, Ishi was eager to please his new friends. He was very courageous about beginning a totally new way of life and adapted well to his new surroundings. For months, he patiently worked with the anthropologists to establish a vocabulary of Yahi words, and eventually he learned a bit of English. He was able during the next few years to describe to the museum staff many aspects of his former way of life and to provide invaluable information about the vanished Yahi world.

One fact about Ishi was never discovered: his real name. He never told the anthropologists—or anyone else—his personal name, for that was not the Yahi custom. Needing some way to refer to him, Alfred Kroeber began to use "Ishi," which means simply "man" in Yahi, and Ishi accepted the name without objection.

Ishi was always willing to share his knowledge of traditional Yahi skills. He did many demonstrations at the museum of such crafts as making fire with a fire drill and making tools and weapons of stone and wood. Ishi knew exactly which natural materials to use to produce knives of razor sharpness, delicate arrow points, and strong bows, arrows, harpoons, and other necessities of Yahi life. He also showed how expertly he could use these items in hunting and fishing, how he tracked and lured and ambushed game animals, and other traditional survival skills.

In the summer of 1914, Ishi was persuaded by Kroeber and Waterman to revisit with them some of the places where he had lived his earlier life. The anthropologists gained a unique opportunity to get a glimpse of Ishi in his native land. But Ishi did not enjoy his return to the wilderness and the painful memories of his hard life there. He was glad when the trip ended and he could go back to the place he had come to consider home—the museum.

Ishi demonstrated traditional Yahi skills for
Kroeber and Waterman during their trip to Ishi's homeland.

Late in the same year, Ishi became ill with tuberculosis. Despite the best available medical attention, he died in March 1916, less than five years after he had walked out of the wilderness to join the modern world.

Ishi's accounts of Yahi lore and demonstrations of Yahi life skills were great contributions to the historical record about American Indians. Yet it was his character that most affected those who were close to him during his years at the museum. Ishi's patience, gentleness, warmth, and sensitivity impressed all who knew him. These qualities were especially remarkable because he had spent most of his lifetime in grief, fear, and deprivation. With Ishi's death, the world lost not only a last contact with a vanished culture, but also one individual's example of the better side of human nature.

ès ès ès ès

Black Elk
Lakota mystic and medicine man
1863?–1950

He was a visionary, a dreamer, and a prophet; a healer and a holy man. He also witnessed some of the most famous events in the late nineteenth-century wars for control of Indian territory. Years later he told his story for publication. It became one of the most important books ever written about Indian spirituality. It was a source of inspiration especially for many non-Indians seeking to understand Indian religious beliefs.

Black Elk was a member of the Oglala band of the Lakota nation. He was born near the eastern end of the border between Wyoming and Montana, at a time when his people were desperately trying to resist the flood of soldiers, settlers, and gold seekers moving into the region. Black Elk's boyhood was like that of any ordinary Oglala youth of that stormy time, except for certain extraordinary mystical experiences he had.

At the age of nine, Black Elk fell unconscious for twelve days, awakening to recall his "Great Vision." This vision changed his life. In it, he seemed to see the future. He was shown a dance ceremony, and he was granted special powers by the Six Grandfathers, who were the spirits of the sky and the earth and the four directions. But the vision and its message so disturbed and frightened young Black Elk that he could not tell anyone for seven years. Guarding his secret inside him, he continued to live a traditional Lakota life.

When Black Elk was thirteen, he was with his second cousin, Crazy Horse, the great Lakota warrior, at the Battle of the Little Bighorn in southern

Montana. In defense of their people, Lakota, Cheyenne, and Arapaho warriors completely wiped out the forces of the U.S. Army's Seventh Cavalry, led by George Armstrong Custer. After the victory—often referred to as Custer's Last Stand—the young Black Elk collected his first scalp from a dying soldier. The American military was embarrassed and enraged by their defeat at the Little Bighorn. Out for revenge, the army poured troops and artillery into the region. Within a year, many Lakota, including Black Elk, had been forced to flee for their lives to Canada.

Black Elk continued to have visions, and his people began to notice that he had unusual powers of understanding. When he was eighteen, a medicine man interpreted his mystical experiences for him. He told Black Elk that he must perform the dance ceremony that he had been told about in his visions. After he carried out these instructions, Black Elk's unusual abilities seemed to increase.

Eventually, Black Elk and the others who had gone to Canada were forced to return to reservations in the United States. In 1886, Black Elk, like many other young Indians, joined the Buffalo Bill Wild West Show. Organized by former scout and Indian fighter William "Buffalo Bill" Cody, this show was an enormously popular form of entertainment. Indians in the show performed traditional songs and dances and demonstrated their skill with bows and arrows.

Black Elk toured Europe for three years with the Wild West Show, visiting England, Italy, Germany, and France. In London, Black Elk performed for Queen Victoria. But in Paris, Black Elk became ill and had another vision experience, one that filled him with anxiety about his people and made him return home immediately.

When he arrived back at the Pine Ridge Reservation in South Dakota, Black Elk found his people miserable and near starvation. But they were placing great hope in the Ghost Dance religion, a religion that promised believers return of the buffalo and a revival of the traditional Indian way of life. Somewhat reluctantly, he participated in the new movement. Months later, it came to a tragic end with the terrible massacre at Wounded Knee. Black Elk was not there to see the killing, but he saw the field not long afterward. The sight of the bloody aftermath saddened and horrified him.

Nearly four decades later, when Black Elk was an old man, the poet John G. Neihardt found him, still at Pine Ridge, an elder respected for his wisdom, healing, and spiritual powers. He still carried great hopes for his people; as he put it, he wanted the Tree of Life to bloom again for them. Neihardt wrote down and edited the story Black Elk told of his experiences, both mystical and historical.

Black Elk (center) and John Neihart (left), the recorder of
Black Elk's historical and mystical experiences

Their collaboration resulted in a literary classic, *Black Elk Speaks; Being the Life Story of a Holy Man of the Oglala Sioux*, first published in 1932. It vividly details the visions of Black Elk. These visions were meant, Black Elk said, to protect the Sioux way of life, despite the disastrous effects of contact with white people. The book also recounted the famous battles he had seen, climaxing with "the end of the dream" at Wounded Knee. Through the years the book became one of the most widely read autobiographical accounts of American Indian life. For millions of non-Indian readers the world over, it has provided their only glimpse of American Indian spirituality.

ơ ơ ơ ơ

Gertrude Simmons Bonnin

Yankton Dakota writer and reformer

1876–1938

I've lost my long hair; my eagle plumes too
For you my own people, I've gone astray . . .
A wanderer now, with no place to stay.
The will-o-wisp learning, it brought me rue . . .

Gertrude Simmons Bonnin felt acutely the pain of loosing her place in the Dakota world without finding a comfortable place in the white world. She did not give in to this pain; her response was to work toward creating a new alliance among the fragmented tribal nations in an intertribal (or pan-Indian) movement for change. Like many reformers at the turn of the century, she saw the pan-Indian movement as the most realistic approach to solving the terrible problems faced by many Indian nations. She used her gift for communication to become one of the movement's most able spokespersons.

Her Dakota name was Zitkala-sa, meaning "Red Bird," and she was born in Greenwood, Nebraska. Records show that Gertrude Simmons was the daughter of a Yankton Dakota mother and a white father. She lived at Yankton Reservation in South Dakota in a Dakota environment until she was eight years old. Then, against her mother's judgment, she followed in the footsteps of her older brother to a Quaker school for Indians in Wabash, Indiana. At the school, she soon discovered how well-intentioned people could bring misery to Indian children through their lack of understanding Indian customs. She returned home three years later, "neither a wild Indian nor a tame one," as she put it, because by then she had begun to absorb the ways of the white people she had been living among.

Several years later, once more against her mother's wishes, she went back to the same school, graduated, and went on to attend Earlham College in Richmond, Indiana. Despite her persistent sense of discomfort and isolation in the white world, she did well in college, winning prizes in oratory contests. Encouraged by this success, she decided she wanted words and ideas to be her life. She would become a professional writer.

That ambition had to wait, but not for long. After leaving Earlham, she taught for two years at Carlisle Indian School, in Pennsylvania. But Gertrude Simmons was also a very talented musician, so she left Carlisle to study violin at a music conservatory in Boston. In 1900, she visited Paris as the leader and violin soloist with the Carlisle Band. Meanwhile, she kept on writing. Several of her stories and autobiographical essays were published in prominent national magazines, and in 1901, her first book, *Old Indian Legends*, was published under her Dakota name, Zitkala-Sa.

Like many educated Indians of that era, Gertrude went to work for the Bureau of Indian Affairs (BIA). In 1902, she married a fellow employee, Raymond T. Bonnin, also Dakota. They soon moved to northwestern Utah, because Raymond was appointed school superintendent on the Uintah and Ouray Reservation. During the fourteen years they lived in Utah, they had a son, and Gertrude worked part-time as a teacher and leader of a musical group.

In 1911, she began corresponding with the Society of American Indians (SAI). The SAI was a reform organization that sought to bring Indians into the mainstream of society while recognizing and preserving Indian uniqueness. SAI members, who were Indians of various tribes, often did not agree on how to achieve their desired goals. But the organization provided an important forum. Their discussions from the Indian viewpoint raised issues that affected all Indians.

Two boys study in the dormitory at Carlisle Indian School in Pennsylvania around 1900.

From this involvement, Gertrude Bonnin developed a new career. In 1916, she was elected secretary of the SAI, and she and her husband moved to Washington, D.C., where the headquarters was located. She acted as its representative to the BIA and edited its magazine. She lectured on Indian rights across the country. After the SAI broke apart in 1926, she founded the National Council of American Indians to carry on with similar aims. She served as its president until her death.

Gertrude Bonnin also began to work with other groups concerned with the welfare of Indians, notably the General Federation of Women's Clubs and the Indian Rights Association. With their sponsorship, she led an investigation of government treatment of tribes, and she tried to influence legislation for better education, health care, and other needed improvements. She persuaded the Federation to support the formation of a special group, the Meriam Commission, to survey living conditions of Indians. The Commission's 1928 report, to which she contributed, led President Herbert Hoover and later President Franklin D. Roosevelt to institute significant reforms in the federal government's Indian policy. With all her activities, Gertrude Bonnin did not write as much as she once had. Her second book, *American Indian Stories* (1921), mainly reprinted earlier publications. She stayed interested in music, and she composed an opera, *Sun Dance*, with William Hanson. For a quarter century, Gertrude Bonnin was ceaselessly occupied with pressing for changes to benefit the larger Indian community. With her intelligence and gift for words, she was an extrordinarily effective lobbyist for Indian rights.

≈ ≈ ≈ ≈

Frank Little
Cherokee labor organizer
1879–1917

During the early 1900s, the Industrial Workers of the World (IWW) was a labor organization dedicated to changing the world. During the early 1900s, the ordinary working people of the world, said its charter, must "take possession of the earth . . . and abolish the wage system." Frank Little, a miner and all-around rebel, was one of the IWW's most dynamic leaders. He traveled throughout the western United States, agitating on behalf of the IWW's kind of unionism, attracting criticism that eventually led to his death.

The son of a Cherokee mother and a Quaker father, Frank Little was known as both a revolutionary and a pacifist. Tough-minded, uncompromising, and fearless, he repeatedly endured terrible beatings and imprisonment to advance the cause he believed in. Little began his working life as a metal miner. Like many miners at the time, he joined the Western Federation of Miners, a craft union active in mining districts across the American West. Sometime around this period of his life he came to believe that the basic structure of American industry must change in rapid and sweeping ways.

In 1906, Little took a job with the newly formed Industrial Workers of the World. The IWW was unlike other trade unions that protected the interests of just one group of craft workers. Instead, the IWW set out to unite "in one big union" all the least skilled and most powerless members of the work force, notably recent immigrants, migrant workers, women, and nonwhites. IWW members, who were often called "Wobblies," wanted to use passive resistance and nonviolent actions, such as strikes, to pressure society into change. The Wobblies aimed to create a new economic system where all the ordinary workers, not just a small group of rich bosses, would each own a piece of the factories, mines, equipment, and other resources used in making products.

To employers with established financial interests in their businesses, this idea seemed like a very threatening challenge. IWW organizers such as Frank Little faced strong opposition, and some of that opposition led to violence against the Wobblies. Nonetheless, Little resolutely involved himself in campaigns for free and open speech about forming unions. In California, he helped organize Mexican and Japanese farmhands and construction workers into a local branch of the IWW. He traveled around organizing harvesters, lumberjacks, and many of his earlier co-workers, the metal miners, as members of the IWW. In 1914, Little was elected to a high office in the IWW leadership. But he didn't want a desk job like that, so he soon went back to traveling to organize local union branches and to participate in strike actions. Tall, wiry, weatherbeaten, and blind in one eye, he was by nature rebellious, forthright, proud of his courage, and always ready for trouble, which often came his way.

In 1914, members of the IWW meet at Union Square, New York City.

In June 1917, a terrible fire occurred in a copper mine near Butte, Montana. One hundred sixty-four miners were trapped and burned to death behind doors that were supposed to be movable, but were not. Outraged mine workers immediately began to strike for safer working conditions. On crutches and in pain because of a recently broken leg, Frank Little arrived in Butte to support the strikers.

At this time, Little was well known as a labor organizer, and strongly disliked by many people. The United States had entered World War I just a few months before, and many people thought of Little's pacifism as treason. When he addressed a crowd of 6,000 at the Butte ballpark, his angry call for drastic change made him powerful enemies.

A few nights later six masked men kicked in the door of the boarding house room where Little was staying. They dragged him from bed to a waiting car, tied him to the bumper, drove the car to a bridge, and hanged him. His vigilante killers were never identified, possibly because no vigorous efforts were made to find them.

Although the lynching and murder of Frank Little did not spark further violence in Butte, his death brought the Wobblies more unfriendly national attention. Public figures increasingly proclaimed the IWW a menace to the nation, and for years Wobblies were persecuted. Yet in later years some of the IWW's philosophy became widely accepted. The tactics of nonviolent confrontation practiced by Wobblies such as Frank Little became an important part of the labor and civil rights movements.

♦ ♦ ♦ ♦

Will Rogers
Cherokee cowboy humorist,
writer, and actor
1879–1935

He was tall and a little stoop-shouldered, with big ears, a wide shy grin, an easy Oklahoma drawl, and a wickedly deft way of poking fun at human foolishness, especially the kind exhibited by politicians. In a few words he could get to the heart of a situation and sum it up with a humor that was pointed but never unkind. Will Rogers' witty commentaries on the public scene kept millions of Americans laughing and hopeful during the bad times of the Depression. He made his reputation as an ordinary commonsense man, but by the time he died, many people thought he was the most influential private citizen in America.

William Penn Adair Rogers was the last son of a prominent part-Cherokee family who owned a ranch near Claremore, Oklahoma. He was very proud of his Cherokee heritage. Years later he told a group of *Mayflower* descendants, "My ancestors met yours when they landed. In fact, they would have showed better judgement if they had not let yours land." In his youth, Will gloried in the vigorous, foot-loose freedom of the last days of the American frontier. He loved the cattle-roping and riding-the-range part of ranch life. Books and classrooms bored him. He attended six schools, and completed the equivalent of high school before his father quit trying to make sure he got an education. Instead, Will excelled at rope tricks with his lasso.

That skill got him into show business, but only by accident. In 1902, he set off with a friend for Argentina, planning to become a gaucho on a ranch there. He wound up in South Africa, in need of a job. Luckily, he encountered the traveling Texas Jack's Wild West Show. When Texas Jack saw him twirl huge rope loops and dance in and out of a spinning lariat, he was immediately hired. Billed as "the Cherokee Kid," rope artist and rough rider, he was an instant hit. Soon he joined a touring circus in Australia and New Zealand, then returned to the United States to perform on the vaudeville circuit.

Will Rogers gradually included more jokes and stories with his rope tricks. He explored the comic possibilities of chewing gum. More and more he played "his natchell self," the shrewd, rumpled, wise innocent. Twirling his rope, he would suddenly lift his candid blue eyes and infectious grin to his audience and quietly make a few homespun observations that raised howls of laughter.

Eventually Rogers dropped the rope part of his act and just talked. In New York in 1916, he joined the most popular stage revue of the time, the Ziegfeld Follies. It was there that he began his famous daily commentaries on the news. Beginning with the line, "All I know is what I read in the papers," he would bring into comic focus whatever was ridiculous in that day's events and personalities. To keep the act up to date, he searched every newspaper for fresh material. Congressmen were especially useful as subjects for humor: "Believe me, I found they are funnier 365 days a year than anything I ever heard of."

Within a few years his jokes were so successful that they were collected in several books. In 1922, Rogers began writing the same kind of material in a popular weekly syndicated newspaper column that he continued until his death. Before long, his column was carried by hundreds of papers across the country, and he regularly reached an estimated 35 million delighted readers. With his unfailing ability to see straight through any hypocrisy in government or big business, he became recognized as a spokesman for the ordinary American. But his jests were gentle enough that no one felt hurt by what he said. Somehow his essential qualities of decency and honesty always came through to people.

Rogers' career developed in several more directions. In 1926, he took his commentary onto the radio, and within a few years was doing a very influential weekly broadcast. He wrote a series of books with the same characteristic Will

A publicity photo of Will Rogers holding the rope he twirled while telling stories and jokes

Rogers touch. He appeared in Broadway shows and in the new medium of sound film, becoming a highly successful movie actor. He starred in at least fifteen movies. His earnings from movies, writing, radio, and lecturing were about $600,000 a year by 1934, making him the highest paid entertainer of his time.

And Rogers was notably generous with his money. He gave cash openhandedly to many charitable and relief organizations. He participated in numerous benefit performances for people displaced by natural disasters or made down-at-the-heel by the Depression. His generosity became legendary, endearing him more to the American heart than anything he ever said.

He lived quite comfortably in Beverly Hills with his family—his wife Betty, his sweetheart from adolescence; and their three children. He was fond of playing polo and owned a stable of polo ponies. He also was an aviation enthusiast. In August 1935, he accompanied Wiley Post, a fellow Oklahoman and a pioneer aviator, on a trip to find a safer route eastward from Alaska. Their one-engine plane developed trouble and plunged into shallow water near Point Barrow, killing them both.

"Live your life," Rogers once said, "so that whenever you lose, you're ahead." The whole nation mourned his passing.

Will Rogers, Jr., also has had a distinguished career, in areas only slightly different from his famous father. He has been a newspaper publisher and lecturer; he has acted in films, including one where he played his father; and he served in the U.S. Congress, something that might have amused his father. Will Rogers, Jr., has also been an active supporter of Indian rights.

❧ ❧ ❧ ❧

Maria Martinez
San Ildefonso Pueblo potter
c.1884–1980

U sing her bare hands and the most humble materials from the desert near her home, Maria Martinez created distinctive works of art so lovely and perfect that she became the most celebrated American Indian maker of pottery. Her fame opened the way for many other artists in her ancient village of San Ildefonso, giving members of the community greater economic security and a renewed interest in Pueblo art.

For hundreds of years, making pottery was part of the work normally done by women living in the pueblos, or villages, of the Southwest. The jars, dishes, vases, and other clay objects that they made were used as ordinary containers and in religious ceremonies. But in the 1800s the Pueblos, the Spanish name for various groups of Indians who live in pueblos, began to rely on manufactured items, especially of metal, to meet some of those needs. By the end of the century, most pottery that Pueblo women made was produced to sell in a growing tourist market.

Maria Montoya grew up in a family where traditional Pueblo ways were cherished and practiced every day. When she was a child she learned the traditional methods of making pottery from her aunt. She learned to knead together certain kinds of local clay with volcanic ash and water, then shape the mixture freehand, coiling long strips of clay up from a base and gradually smoothing the clay into a balanced form. After air drying, the clay object was often painted with designs before being fired, or baked in an oven, to harden it.

Maria was patient and hard-working, and she became very quick and skillful at shaping pots that were thin-walled, symmetrical, and exceptionally beautiful.

Her village of San Ildefonso, just north of Santa Fe, New Mexico, was a poor community. Most of the income came from farming. By the time she was a young woman, Maria's ability to produce pots to sell in the Santa Fe market was becoming a real asset to her family.

In 1904, she married Julian Martinez, a young artist from her pueblo who was to become her partner in making pottery for the rest of his life. Julian took a job at the Museum of New Mexico in Santa Fe. Maria began to visit the museum exhibits and became familiar with examples of ancient Pueblo pottery. An archeologist at the museum who heard of her pottery-making skills asked Maria about some fragments of an unknown type of shiny black pottery he had excavated. Although she had previously made only polychrome, or multicolored, pottery, she and Julian set to work to figure out how the ancient black pottery had been made. After researching and experimenting, they came upon a method of firing the clay that reproduced the dark lustrous finish. It became their specialty, and through several decades they made hundreds of pieces of their easily recognized "San Ildefonso blackware."

On the left is an example of Maria Martinez's black pottery and on the right her polychrome pottery.

Their collaboration also included many fine pieces of polychrome pottery. Julian had a gift for creating designs and for painting his crisp, striking decorations onto the clay of both polychrome pottery and blackware. Yet it was the blackware that won them international recognition and a measure of financial success. Museums and individual buyers were eager to acquire everything Maria and Julian could make. They won awards in many art shows and were asked to demonstrate their techniques at expositions across the United States.

Maria and Julian had to work very hard to keep up with the demand for their wares. In time, other members of the family, including several of their children, began to help. Pottery-making became a flourishing industry in San Ildefonso, and it has remained so. A remarkable number of their family members have become acclaimed potters and artists in their own right; some continuing in well-established styles, others exploring new approaches to clay and painting.

In 1943, Julian Martinez died. At first Maria felt too sad to continue working, but after a while she resumed making superb pottery in collaboration with other family members. A daughter-in-law, Santana Martinez, painted decorations on some of her work. Later, Maria worked with her son Popovi Da, a distinguished painter, potter, and silver jewelry maker known for his artistic innovations. Together they revived traditional polychrome pottery and also used a beautiful blackware finish that made Maria's pottery seem to glow with a silver light.

Even in her frail nineties, Maria continued to make pottery. Her honors never changed her quiet commitment to the traditions of the small community in which she lived. In San Ildefonso, she was deeply respected, partly for the renown her work brought to the Pueblos, but also as an important link between the modern world and the valued past, and a clear proof of the vitality of the ancestral ways. For Maria Martinez, making pottery was how she expressed who she was and where she belonged.

The Indian Reorganization and Citizenship Acts

Historically U.S. laws and policies toward American Indian nations have hampered the development of Indian rights and interests. The General Allotment Act or Dawes Act of 1887 was especially disastrous for Indian cultures. The Dawes Act, which attempted to turn Indians into farmers by setting individuals up with their own plots of land, or allotments, actually separated Indians from much of their land holdings. The allotment policy also broke up traditional social and community relationships.

By the early 1920s, the disastrous effects of allotment were quite clear and a movement to reverse it was underway. Fueling that movement was the Meriam Report, issued in 1928. The Meriam Report was the findings of a study by a committee of highly respected researchers, and it shocked the nation with details of the dismal living conditions on reservations. It was a major reason why in 1934 Congress passed the Indian Reorganization Act (IRA), also called the Wheeler-Howard Act. The IRA was an attempt to correct the wrongs of the previous half-century by reducing federal control of Indian affairs and restoring Indian nations' self-government and self-determination.

One of the chief forces behind the IRA was John Collier, the Commissioner of Indian Affairs from 1933 to 1945 and for many more years a central figure in Indian policy matters. He was deeply committed to promoting social justice and developed many reform proposals. Unfortunately, only a few of his recommendations were included in the IRA.

The IRA gave tribes the possibility of making reforms in three major areas. First, the IRA was intended to stop the loss of the Indian land base. The Dawes Act was repealed, thus ending allotment. The IRA provided for the return of surplus unallotted lands to tribal control, rather than letting them be sold off to homesteaders as before. It also set up a fund that could be used to buy more reservation land.

Second, some parts of the IRA sought to promote participation by Indians in their reservation's internal political and economic affairs. The IRA encouraged tribes to adopt written constitutions and charters. It provided money to help tribes organize governmental bodies and form corporations for managing tribal property.

The third major area of reform in the IRA concerned jobs and education. It established a fund that would make educational loans available to Indian students. It also said that qualified Indians would be given preference for jobs in the Bureau of Indian Affairs.

In 1935, John Collier (standing), Commissioner of Indian Affairs, watched as Secretary of the Interior Ickes signed the constitution for the Flathead from Montana.

Members of each nation could vote on whether they wanted the IRA applied to them. Nations were granted a period in which to debate whether to accept the IRA. When they finally voted, 181 Indian nations, representing about 130,000 people, decided to accept, and 77 nations, representing more than 86,000 people, decided to reject the IRA. Fourteen others did not vote and were automatically included. Within twelve years, 161 nations adopted constitutions and 131 groups (not all were tribes) adopted charters.

As the voting results suggest, Indian response to the IRA was mixed. Each nation brought a different set of needs and viewpoints to the IRA question. In many nations only a small minority of people voted.

The reasons for not wanting the IRA varied. For some groups, local bands or villages were important to their people, but not the organization of the whole tribe. To some groups, the kind of democracy proposed in the IRA was just too different from their traditional way of conducting civic affairs. Other groups had managed to do well enough under allotment that they did not want to change that system. They had mingled enough in the white world that they did not want to return to a more traditional tribal existence.

To many observers, in later years especially, an underlying problem with the IRA was that it brought another series of attempts to impose on Indians the values and ideals of the white society. The IRA gave the U.S. Secretary of the Interior a great deal of power in deciding how to carry out the law. Most Indian constitutions that were adopted under the IRA were modeled on suggestions made by federal officials, not Indian sources. The effect of this was that the conduct of tribal government was being determined by white institutions and attitudes.

It was John Collier's idea of reform that became the basis of the IRA. Thus, to a degree, the IRA's shortcomings represented the limitations of his understanding. Still, on balance, the IRA was a real improvement for Indians, because it ended allotment. In the long run it contributed significantly to the revitalization of Indian life. Many of Collier's other reforms never came about. By the middle 1940s, his sympathetic approach to Indian policy was falling out of public favor.

John Collier shortly after being sworn in as Commissioner of Indian Affairs in 1933

Besides, money for his programs dried up with the coming of World War II. Nonetheless, the IRA continued to be the key part of federal Indian policy for many years.

In 1924, ten years before the IRA, Congress passed the Indian Citizenship Act, another major law affecting American Indians. It extended U.S. and state citizenship to all noncitizen Indians. At the time, many Indians were already citizens. Some had previously received citizenship under terms of a treaty or the Dawes Act, through service in the military in World War I, by marriage of Indian women to U.S. citizens, or under other arrangements.

Citizenship was not the same as the right to vote, however. State laws, not the U.S. Congress, determined who was eligible to vote, so in some cases voting rights took more time to secure. In some states there were discriminating laws preventing voting rights for Indians as late as 1948.

When the Citizenship Act was first passed, it made little difference to many Indians, because they had no opportunity to learn about and take advantage of their new status. But a decade later, when the IRA opened up more possibilities for Indian self-determination, some people became interested in white civic affairs, the rights and privileges of citizenship, and voting. Since the civil rights movement in the 1960s, Americans have broadened their understanding of the rights and privileges of citizenship. Now American Indians are sharing in some aspects of the larger American political process.

Clarence L. Tinker
Osage major general,
U.S. Army Air Corps
1887–1942

The surprise Japanese attack on the naval base at Pearl Harbor on December 7, 1941, was a terrible disaster for the American military. The base was not prepared for an assault. The huge loss of American lives, ships, and aircraft stirred up a storm of criticism, and several top commanders were fired as a result.

The new leader put in charge of turning the tattered remains of the Air Corps in Hawaii into a fighting force for the Pacific was Clarence Tinker, an Osage bomber pilot with roots in Oklahoma. The excellent discipline and training of the Air Corps at the Battle of Midway the following summer is a testimony to how well he did the task. Sadly, however, Tinker died in that battle.

Clarence Leonard Tinker was born in Edgin, Kansas, in 1887, near the border of the Osage Nation of Indian Territory. Although by birth he was only one-eighth Osage, his childhood was greatly influenced by that part of his ancestry. He was an enrolled member of the Osage Nation, learned the Osage language, attended an Osage boarding school, and was surrounded by people who valued their Osage heritage. His father was the publisher of the first Osage newspaper.

Clarence Tinker's high school years were spent at the Haskell Institute for Indians in Kansas. Then, in 1906, members of the Osage tribe began receiving shares of the profits from oil and mineral resources mined on Osage lands. Clarence felt his future was more financially secure, so he decided to explore the world. He enrolled in Wentworth Military Academy in Lexington, Missouri, to acquire a good grounding for a career in military service. His first job upon graduation was with the police force in the Philippine Islands, which were then under American control. He took to the job, which brought him a taste of danger while pursuing armed bandits and the adventure of learning about a new culture. It was his first posting to a faraway place in a career that eventually required him and his family to move many times.

Tinker received a commission in the U.S. army in 1912. Soon the new second lieutenant was sent to a post near Honolulu, Hawaii, where he met and married a visiting Canadian, Madeline Doyle. In time, Clarence and Madeline had three children.

By 1919, Tinker had become fascinated with airplanes and with flying them. He took a few flying lessons on his own, and on the strength of his obvious natural ability was admitted to the Pilot School of the recently formed Army Air Service. Thus began his career as an army aviator, with growing responsibilities related to training new aviators.

As Tinker gained experience, he was steadily promoted up the ranks. Within a few years he was transferred to a long series of assignments, including duty in Arizona, California, Texas, Oklahoma, Kansas, Virginia, Washington, D.C., Florida, and England.

In 1926, at an air field near London, England, he and another flier crashed while on a routine flight. Painfully injured, Tinker still managed to drag the other man free of the burning wreckage before he collapsed unconscious. For his bravery, Major Tinker was awarded the Soldier's Medal, the country's highest peacetime honor.

From the beginning of his flying career, Tinker had a reputation for caring about the welfare of the men in his command, for being sometimes strict and exacting, and for always being very capable. Tall, slim, and sinewy, he liked to look trim and neat at all times. Even with their frequent moves, he and Madeline enjoyed an active social life. They often invited other officers to their home for dinner.

By 1940, when Tinker was promoted to brigadier general, the army was in the process of responding to the growing threat of war. Among the masses of new equipment that U.S. factories were producing to get ready for war were bombers. Tinker, the highly skilled pioneer pilot, was more and more concerned with training bomber crews and planning just how the big planes might be used.

Planes burn and men stare in shock after the surprise Japanese attack on Pearl Harbor, Hawaii.

When word came of the Pearl Harbor attack and the shake-up in military leadership that followed, Tinker was ready. In January 1942, he was promoted to major general, becoming the highest-ranking American Indian in the army. Tinker foresaw that air power would be decisive in the war, and he set about reorganizing the Air Corps at Hawaii into a highly disciplined fighting unit. He also began planning for the events we remember today as the Battle of Midway. Midway, in early June 1942, was fought almost entirely with aircraft. The battle was the turning point in the Pacific war; it ended the threat of further invasions by the Japanese.

General Tinker did not live to understand the full significance of the battle he helped to plan. On June 7, while leading a bomber squadron on a combat mission about thirty miles from Midway Island, his plane was suddenly lost from sight. He and his crew were never found.

Tinker was the first army general to die in action in World War II. After his death, he was awarded the Distinguished Service Medal by the U.S. government. In Oklahoma, the Osage Nation honored him with a special victory dance and ceremonies attended by hundreds of people. A new air field near Oklahoma City was soon named after him. Today, it is known as Tinker Air Force Base.

᠀ ᠀ ᠀ ᠀

Jim Thorpe
Sac and Fox Olympic athlete
1888–1953

Jim Thorpe was a sports champion who could do it all. Competing in the Olympics, he accomplished something no one else has ever done—he won both the pentathlon and decathlon. He played pro baseball in the summer and pro football in the winter; he was exceptionally good at track, hockey, lacrosse, boxing, and swimming. In recognition of his athletic excellence and versatility he was named the best American male athlete and best football player of the first half of the twentieth century.

James Francis Thorpe was born in central Oklahoma (known then as Indian Territory). His parents, who were Sac and Fox, owned a 160-acre farm near their tribe's reservation land. Jim had a twin, Charles, and the brothers were very close. Happiest when they were active and outdoors, they hunted, fished, and trapped together, and they wrestled and raced each other.

When they were six, Jim and Charles began attending the boarding school on the reservation. A couple of winters later Charles developed pneumonia and died. This early tragedy in Jim's life upset him deeply. Without his brother and companion, Jim became very quiet and shy; he lost interest in school activities. Finally he ran away from school and returned to his family's farm.

When he was eleven, Jim went to the Haskell Institute in Kansas, a government boarding school for Indians. There he discovered football and his great talent for the game. But family tragedy struck again. His father was injured in an accident, and a short time later his mother died unexpectedly. Jim left Haskell and never returned.

After working on the family farm for several years, Jim enrolled at the age of sixteen at the Carlisle Indian School in Carlisle, Pennsylvania. The football coach, the great Glenn "Pop" Warner, recognized Jim's abilities. He helped Jim to develop a wide range of athletic skills, especially those needed for track and field contests.

A natural at track events, Jim Thorpe began to win as soon as he began to compete. At a series of track meets during the 1907 season, he won the high and broad jumps, the shot put, and the high and low hurdles. Jim wanted to play varsity football too.

Jim Thorpe throws the discus in 1913.

In the 1908 season, he was ready for football. Jim's phenomenal running, passing, and kicking enabled the Carlisle team to defeat the best college teams of the day, including Army and the University of Pennsylvania. He and his tiny school were suddenly famous. In 1911 and 1912, he was named halfback on the All-America team.

At Carlisle, Jim proved to be a fine all-around athlete. He especially enjoyed baseball and spent several summer vacations playing the game just "because I liked to play ball."

In 1912, Jim competed at the Olympic games at Stockholm, Sweden. He won four of the five events in the pentathlon and topped all previous records in the decathlon, scoring 8,412 out of a possible 10,000 points. For this feat, the King of Sweden called him "the greatest athlete in the world."

But a few months later Jim suffered a setback that darkened the rest of his life. Olympic contestants were expected to be completely unpaid amateurs in sports; it turned out that one summer Jim had accepted $15 a week to play baseball. Jim never denied he had been paid. He explained that in taking the money he had been "a schoolboy, not wise to the ways of the world," and unaware of the rules about money. Nevertheless, the Amateur Athletic Union took away his Olympic medals and removed his name from the official records.

For the next six years Jim played professional baseball for three National League teams. He was an excellent runner and outfielder, and a good batter in general. He was more successful at football, which he played professionally for various teams, from 1915 to 1929. He was the spectacular star of the Canton (Ohio) Bulldogs in 1922 and 1923, leading them in two undefeated seasons. He also helped to found the organization that became the National Football League.

After he retired from professional sports in 1929, Jim tried a number of jobs, but he never seemed to find the right one. He had a few small parts in movies, did a lecture tour and made celebrity appearances, and briefly joined the merchant marine during World War II. He returned to Oklahoma to speak out in favor of changing the Sac and Fox tribal constitution, which many people felt

Jim Thorpe plays baseball with two of his sons, Phillip (at bat) and Billie (at right).

gave too much power to the federal government.

For the most part, Jim lived his later years in relative obscurity, and he saw some hard times. He was troubled by alcoholism. He married three times and had eight children, one of whom died in his arms. Unlike many athletes of today, he never made a great amount of money, either during his sports career or afterwards.

Not long before the end of his life, Jim was back in the news. In 1950, two Associated Press polls of sports writers selected him the best athlete and best football player for 1900–1950. A year later a major motion picture of his life, *Jim Thorpe: All-American*, was released.

Other recognition of his achievements came after his death. In 1954, two Pennsylvania towns joined together to become the town of Jim Thorpe, Pennsylvania. In 1973, sixty years after he was stripped of his Olympic honors, the American Athletic Union declared that Jim Thorpe had been an amateur in 1913 after all. Finally, in 1982, after ceaseless efforts by his children to get back Thorpe's Olympic medals, the International Olympic Committee reinstated Jim Thorpe as cowinner of the 1912 pentathlon and decathlon.

The Delorias

Ella Cara Deloria
Yankton Dakota linguist and anthropologist
1889–1971

Vine Deloria, Sr.
Yankton Dakota priest
1901–1990

Phillip Sam Deloria
Dakota attorney
19–?

Vine Deloria, Jr.
Dakota writer and activist
1939–

Two centuries ago, in France, the dropping of a guillotine blade made an orphan of a boy named Phillipe Des Lauriers. The boy came to America, and when he grew up, he became a fur trader in the West and married a young Yankton Dakota woman. Their son became a famous medicine man and chief of the Yankton Dakota. Their grandson, Phillip, converted to Christianity and became an Episcopal priest and missionary among the Dakota/Lakota. He changed the family name to Deloria. The Deloria family has, over the generations, included some remarkable individuals. They have been prominent clergymen, scholars, and leaders, and they are to this day making significant contributions to the Indian nations.

One outstanding member of the Deloria family was Ella Cara Deloria. She spent many years studying Dakota language and culture. Ella was the daughter of Phillip Deloria, who was the first Episcopal minister and missionary in the family. She grew up at St. Elizabeth's Mission, among mainly Lakota, on the Standing Rock Reservation in South Dakota. Ella grew up in a home where her Dakota language and culture were valued equally with the ways of white society.

Ella Deloria attended Episcopal schools in South Dakota. A scholarship took her to Oberlin College in Ohio, and then to Columbia University in New York.

Ella Deloria

After graduating in 1915, she taught in an Indian school and she also cared for ailing family members and her younger brother and sister. In 1927, the distinguished anthropologist Franz Boas, whom she had met at Columbia, asked her to work with him researching the Dakota language and culture. So she resigned from her teaching job and embarked on the work that would occupy her for the rest of her life.

Deloria did field research when she could, traveling to Dakota and Lakota reservations to interview elders and gather information. She also edited and translated written texts. She sent the material that she assembled to Boas, and after his death in 1942, to Ruth Benedict, another anthropologist who was his colleague. Deloria's work resulted in several books: *Dakota Texts*, a landmark collection of traditional tales; *Dakota Grammar*; and *Speaking of Indians*, an account of Dakota life. Deloria also wrote *Waterlily*, a novel in which she recreated Indian life from a woman's point of view, but the book was not published until long after her death.

By the 1940s, Ella Deloria had become a recognized authority on the Dakota language and culture. She was devoted to her work, and she continued her research, writing, consulting, and lecturing throughout her later years. During the period 1955 to 1958, she also served as director of her old mission school, St. Elizabeth's.

Deloria's income was small, which sometimes made it hard for her to carry out her work. Somehow, she still managed to gather a very full record of Dakota language and customs. She took great pains to be completely accurate and objective in her work, and the information she made available to the world is considered invaluable.

Vine Deloria, Sr., Ella's cousin, grew up around the same time that she did and eventually became a fountain of knowledge about Indian philosophy, history, and spirituality. Born on the Standing Rock Reservation in 1901, Vine Deloria grew up in a traditional Indian household. Life changed considerably for Vine when, at age sixteen, his mother died.

He attended the Carney Military Academy in Nebraska and St. Stevens College in New York. For a brief time he was a coal miner and then an advisor at the Fort Sill Indian School in Oklahoma. After graduating from the General Theological Seminary in New York and becoming an Episcopalian priest, Vine ministered to people on the Pine Ridge and Sisseton-Wahpeton Reservations. He spent three years at a parish in Denison, Iowa, and then served as General Secretary for Indian Work at the National Episcopal Church in New York City.

Believing that the Episcopal Church should attend to the material needs of Indians, Vine Deloria raised money in the 1930s and 1940s to support Indian causes. In the 1950s, efforts to persuade the Episcopal Church to take a position against the termination of Indian nations severely strained his relationship with the church. Deloria was widely respected for his vast knowledge of Dakota and Lakota traditions and for his impeccable use of the Lakota language. He died in 1990 in Tucson, Arizona.

Deloria's son, Vine Deloria, Jr., is a writer, lawyer, educator, and an advocate of Indian rights. With wit and sometimes biting satire, he has provided insight into relations between Indians and whites, Indian religion, and other Indian issues. He is the author and editor of numerous books and articles.

Vine Deloria, Jr., grew up in South Dakota on the Pine Ridge Reservation but is an enrolled member of the Standing Rock Sioux Tribe. He originally intended to follow the family tradition and become a minister. He attended Iowa State University and graduated in 1958, spent two years in the Marines, and entered the Augustana Lutheran Seminary in Illinois. In 1963, he received his degree in theology, but he decided against becoming a minister.

Deloria became executive director of the National Congress of American Indians (NCAI), an organization of Indian nations. He has said that in his three years at NCAI he learned more than he had in the previous thirty years of his life. He became familiar with the complex economic, social, political, and legal problems facing tribes and the conflicting views on how to resolve the problems. Deloria became convinced that what Indian leaders needed was more legal skills to help them assert their rights and shape their own future. He left NCAI and attended law school at the University of Colorado, graduating in 1970.

In 1969, his first book was published, and it was a best seller. *Custer Died for Your Sins: An Indian Manifesto* was an angry, witty, and brilliant account of the contemporary American Indian situation. It challenged stereotypes, ridiculed various kinds of foolishness, and set forth a vision of Indian survival in the United States: "We are a people unified by our humanity—not a pressure group unified for conquest. And from our greater strength we shall wear down the white man and finally outlast him. . . . We shall endure." More books followed, among them *God Is Red* (1973), contrasting Christianity and Indian religions; and *Behind the Trail of Broken Treaties* (1974), about treaties between Indian nations and the U.S. government.

Since the mid-1970s, Vine Deloria, Jr., has focused his work on issues related to federal law and political science. He was a professor of political science at the University of Arizona for twelve years and since 1990 has been teaching at the University of Colorado.

Phillip Sam Deloria, the second son of Vine Deloria, Sr., and a member of the Standing Rock Sioux tribe is a prominent attorney and director of the American Indian Law Center at the University of New Mexico, School of Law, in Albuquerque. Since 1972, he has assisted more than 1,000 Indian students preparing to enter law schools. In 1974, he helped organize the World Council of Indigenous Peoples—the first international organization of its kind. As Secretary General of the World Council of Indigenous Peoples, Deloria is the first American Indian with official diplomatic recognition at the United Nations. He has also been an advisor to such organizations as the National Tribal Chairmen's Association and the National Congress of American Indians.

Vine Deloria, Jr.'s book Custer Died for Your Sins *had a deep and powerful impact on the American public.*

Frank Fools Crow
Oglala Lakota spiritual leader
1890–1989

In his nearly century of life, Frank Fools Crow witnessed many difficult changes affecting his people, the Lakota. The mission of his life was to preserve the ancient traditions of his people, and heal and help all who sincerely wanted his assistance. He was one of the most prominent and respected medicine men, a holy man. Frank Fools Crow was also the highest ranking civil chief of all the Lakota.

Frank Fools Crow was an Oglala, a member of one of the seven bands of the Lakota Nation. He was born on the Pine Ridge Reservation in South Dakota, near the site of the 1890 massacre at Wounded Knee. His uncle, Black Elk, was the reknowned Lakota spiritual leader and an important influence on his life.

Frank Fools Crow never completed a formal education. Instead, he received nearly all his knowledge in the traditional ways from his family and elders of the tribe. About the time he was thirteen, he began to feel strongly that he was supposed to become a medicine man. His father took him to talk with a well-respected holy man, who directed him on his first vision quest and began to instruct him in the sacred ways.

Among the Lakota, a medicine man or medicine woman is given power to heal, often by using herbs, from *Wakan Tanka*, the highest and most holy One. A holy man or woman possesses not only the power to heal, but also other unusual powers and abilities, often including the ability to foretell the future and interpret messages from the spirit world. Different people have different powers, which are not easy to explain, but are felt by everyone.

Historically, these spiritual leaders were very important in the fabric of Lakota society. During the late nineteenth and early twentieth centuries, however, traditional religious ceremonies held on reservations were forbidden and condemned by those who did not understand them. Consequently, many ceremonies and customs could only be observed in secret. Fortunately, in more recent times many of the ancient ways have been brought back into the open, having been cherished and carefully preserved by spiritual people such as Frank Fools Crow.

In his youth, Frank learned many things about the religious traditions of his people. But he also observed and participated in reservation life and the wider world. When he was fourteen, he made his first long trip, traveling by train to Salt Lake City to take part in a traditional dancing contest. Later he competed in other contests, rode in horse races, held a job as a telephone lineman, and toured the country with a Wild West show. In 1921, he went to Europe for thirteen months as part of a show.

As young Frank learned from the places and people he encountered, his abilities and renown as a medicine man increased also. By the middle 1920s, he was recognized as an important leader in his community and was named a civil chief. During the difficult years from the 1930s through World War II, his reputation as a healer steadily grew. By about 1960, Frank Fools Crow's life had settled into the pattern he kept to for the rest of his life. He conducted special ceremonies for curing sick and disabled people, especially those suffering paralysis, and he regularly conducted traditional religious ceremonies in the Lakota territory.

He was recognized as an elder statesman of the tribe. People came from far and wide to seek information and advice from him. He was invited to many public events, both on and off the reservation. He appeared on radio and television. He traveled to Washington, D.C., to represent the Lakota nation in its plea to government officials for the return of the Black Hills, their traditional sacred lands. In 1973, when members of the American Indian Movement

Well into his 90s, Frank Fools Crow worked to keep his people's native religion alive for future generations.

protested government policies by occupying the town of Wounded Knee, he was part of a delegation trying to reach a peaceful settlement.

Frank Fools Crow was named Ceremonial Chief of the Lakota Nation. This title was conferred on him by general consent, not by election, and carried both the greatest honor and the broadest leadership responsibility.

In the course of Frank Fools Crow's long life, the Lakota coped with many new and troublesome dilemmas. They adjusted to living on ever-shrinking reservations and adapted partially to modern technology. They fought new and difficult social problems, such as discrimination and widespread substance abuse. Oppression and the stress of change sometimes blocked native religion from public sight. But it remained alive in people such as Frank Fools Crow, who safeguarded it for the future.

Te Ata
Chickasaw folklore interpreter and storyteller
1897–

Her name means "bearer of the morning." For thousands of people across the United States, Canada, and Europe, Te Ata, a Chickasaw, has been the bearer of a rich American Indian oral tradition. In a career spanning more than six decades, her dramatic one-woman stage presentations brought many people their first experience of folklore. Te Ata combined stories, song, dance, and pantomime in performances that audiences found both enchanting and deeply moving. She has made a film, created a children's book, and remained active into her nineties. The Chickasaw Nation has honored her for her contributions, and the state of Oklahoma has declared her a "living treasure."

For a century and a half, the Chickasaw people have been living in southern Oklahoma. It was there, near the small town of Tishomingo, that Te Ata, or Mary Thompson, was born in a family of nine children. Her father, Thomas Benjamin Thompson, a Chickasaw, owned a general merchandise store. Her part-Osage mother, Lucy Freund Thompson, was known in the local community for her knowledge of herbal medicine.

In her childhood, Te Ata was surrounded by people who kept their Indian heritage and helped her learn about it. Her mother taught her about using plants to heal sick people. Her father was the one who introduced her to many traditional stories. The first school she attended was an Indian day school. Later she went to a tribal boarding school. When she was little, she liked sports and loved the outdoors. She liked the woods so much that she wanted to become a forester.

Te Ata attended Oklahoma College for Women, becoming its first Indian graduate. In college, she discovered how good she was at storytelling. Just to be entertaining, she told her friends the stories she had heard from her father. A teacher realized that her abilities as a storyteller were exceptional and encouraged her to do more.

After college, she studied at the Theater School of the Carnegie Institute of Technology, in Pittsburgh, Pennsylvania, and then took private lessons to polish her speaking style and stage presence. Within a short time she landed acting jobs in New York on the Broadway stage, including a role as Andromache

Te Ata's great skill for interpreting native stories touched audiences around the world.

in the classic Greek drama *The Trojan Women*. She also appeared in various small theater productions around the country.

Eventually, Te Ata developed her own repertoire weaving together traditional Indian stories, poetry, and music. Her performances were based on what she had known since childhood, together with folklore materials she encountered at folk festivals and studied in courses at schools and museums. Her travels took her to every state in the United States and several European countries.

Te Ata's performances were highly expressive and intensely dramatic. She was widely greeted with acclaim by critics, who noted especially the captivating quality of her voice and her beautiful appearance. She was tall and slender, her gestures were fluidly graceful, and she wore Indian attire, sometimes with blue butterflies in her jet-black hair.

Te Ata's audiences included many well-known people. She was chosen by Eleanor and Franklin D. Roosevelt to represent the American Indian people in a program in New York for the visiting King and Queen of England. She also performed at the White House for President and Mrs. Roosevelt and groups of their guests.

In 1932, Eleanor Roosevelt named Lake Te Ata, near Bear Mountain, New York, in her honor. In 1957, she was honored at the Chickasaw Centennial celebration and inducted into the Oklahoma Hall of Fame. Later, the governor of Oklahoma proclaimed her the first Oklahoma State Treasure in recognition of her years as an advocate and example of an important part of the state's heritage. Diverse groups, from the Girl Scouts to the magazine *Ladies Home Journal* to television's *Today* show, have recognized her contributions toward advancing American Indian oral traditions.

Throughout her career, Te Ata says, she has wanted the Chickasaw and Indians everywhere to be proud of her. She has worked hard to be worthy of their respect and admiration. Clearly she has earned both in full measure.

Ben Reifel
Brule Lakota
U.S. Congressman
1906–1990

Ben Reifel began life in 1906 as a poor boy in a backcountry log cabin built by his father. But there was something inside him that drove him to seek a different future from the one that seemed laid out before him. He knew instinctively that education could open up his future. In time, education let him enter the world beyond the reservation to build an outstanding record of accomplishment and service in government.

Ben Reifel's people were the Brule Sioux, one of the seven bands of the Lakota. He was born on South Dakota's Rosebud Reservation, where his family had a small farm. The land was not very productive, so the family's life was one of hard work and difficulty. They lived as much as possible in accordance with the ways of their ancestors, so very little English was spoken at home. Ben's father felt that the reservation school would not help his children much in the life they were likely to lead. Besides, children had to stay home to help on the farm if the family was to survive. Ben stayed out of school so much that he didn't complete the eighth grade until he was sixteen.

His father did not want him to go on to high school. Ben worked on the farm for three years more, but he had the feeling that the old ways were hurting his chances for a good future. He craved learning about the the rest of the world, because it might show him how to make something better. Finally he ran away to high school. The school was hundreds of miles from his home, and his father did not try to bring him back.

Ben Reifel was a very good student. He went on to college at South Dakota State University, where he studied agriculture—a field he hoped would most benefit people struggling to farm on the reservations. In 1933, he was employed by the Bureau of Indian Affairs (BIA) as the farm agent on the Pine Ridge Reservation in South Dakota.

In 1931, Ben Reifel had been commissioned a second lieutenant in the U.S. Army Reserve. When World War II came, he was ordered to active duty. He served in Europe until 1946, when he was discharged as a lieutenant colonel. He returned to work at several BIA posts, but he soon decided that he needed more education to carry out the kinds of programs he felt were necessary. On scholarships to Harvard University, he received first a master's degree in public administration and then, in 1952, a doctorate, thus becoming one of very few American Indians at that time who had a Ph.D.-level degree.

Congressman and Mrs. Reifel hang one of his diplomas from Harvard University in their home in Aberdeen, South Dakota.

Ben Reifel is sworn in as the first American Indian member of Congress by Speaker of the House Sam Rayburn.

Reifel returned to work for the BIA as superintendent of the Fort Berthold Indian Agency in North Dakota, and then in 1955 was appointed director of the Aberdeen, South Dakota, Area Office of the BIA. This important position made him responsible for the activities of BIA offices and government-operated reservation schools in North and South Dakota and Nebraska, states with large Indian populations.

In this job, Ben continued to feel that Indians must take a hard look at their lives and adapt some of their cultural patterns to the requirements of the present and especially the future. Not everyone agreed—many people thought they should not have to give up traditional ways to meet the outside world's demands. But Reifel believed prosperity and improved living conditions would come with changes such as better school systems and industrial development in Indian country. "We cannot go back to the buffalo economy," he said, "we want a modern standard of living the same as whites."

In 1960, he resigned from the BIA and ran as a Republican for a South Dakota seat in the U.S. Congress. He won easily, and as a congressman he worked hard to secure economic benefits for his district. After five terms in Washington, he retired in 1971, at the age of 65. In later years, he served on a number of boards and commissions, including the National Capitol Planning Commission and the National Advisory Council on Education of Disadvantaged Children.

Judging from the recognition Ben Reifel received for his contributions to the American Indian community, many people were glad that years before, the boy from the Rosebud Reservation ran away to get an education. Among his numerous honors were the Outstanding American Indian Award; the Indian Council Fire Award; several awards from the Boy Scouts of America; the Department of the Interior's highest honor, the Distinguished Service Award; and several honorary doctoral degrees.

ﮭ ﮭ ﮭ ﮭ

The Wests

W. Richard (Dick) West, Sr.
Cheyenne painter, sculptor
1912–

W. Richard West, Jr.
Cheyenne museum director, attorney
1943–

When Richard West, Jr., was very young, he went with his parents to visit a famous natural history museum in New York City. The family was interested in seeing the displays about the native peoples of North America, especially their own tribe, the Cheyenne. But after hours of touring the collections, the little boy had to ask a question. "Why did they put Indians in a museum, next to extinct animals like dinosaurs and mammoths?" His father replied, "I believe they must think we, too, are dead."

Today Richard West, Jr., is working to make sure that visitors get the right impression at the United States' biggest museum devoted to native peoples. West is the director of the newly formed National Museum of the American Indian. He sees the new museum as a splendid opportunity to present native cultures as they really are: complex, contemporary, and alive, not an assortment of frozen moments from the past.

West and his staff have an enormous job figuring out how best to accomplish this. Fortunately, they have a lot of exhibit materials to work with, and when everything is finished, they will have plenty of space. The core of the museum will be a distinguished collection of about a million objects from all over North, Central, and South America, assembled during the first half of this century. Although the museum was officially established in 1989, some of its buildings will not be ready to use until the late 1990s. There will be a branch of

Pictured above: W. Richard (Dick) West, Sr.

the museum in New York City, but most of the artifacts will be kept in new buildings at the Smithsonian Institution in Washington, D.C.

Visitors will be able to see examples of both fine arts and ordinary items crafted for everyday use. They will also see many one-of-a-kind objects, such as Geronimo's hat and Sitting Bull's drum. In addition to artifacts, West wants visitors to encounter Indian dance, drama, music, literature, and other living cultural experiences. He would like to have cultural representatives from various tribes available to talk to visitors, to further show the connection between native cultures and contemporary America.

Richard West, Jr., is a member of the Cheyenne-Arapaho Tribes of Oklahoma. He was born in Muskogee, Oklahoma, in 1943. His father is a noted artist and teacher. Although his mother was non-Indian, she supported his interest in his native heritage. While he was growing up, West was very aware of the elements of Cheyenne culture—art especially—but also Cheyenne history, ceremonial life, and oral tradition. He recalls bedtime stories that were traditional Cheyenne tales, and dancing at local gatherings.

W. Richard (Dick) West, Jr.

In college and afterwards in a graduate program, West studied American history, with an emphasis on American Indian history. He planned to be a college professor, but ultimately he decided to become an attorney. After graduating from Stanford University School of Law he worked for law firms that represented Indian organizations and tribes before courts, the federal government, and Congress.

Richard West, Jr.'s, activities seem to grow naturally out of a background influenced by Richard (Dick) West, Sr. Dick West is one of the most versatile and significant native artists to achieve prominence since World War II. He has used a variety of styles and techniques, from painting with watercolors to sculpting wood.

"Cheyenne Winter Games" by W. Richard (Dick) West

Dick West is famous especially for paintings that depict the life of the Cheyenne during the nineteenth century, including ceremonies, costumes, historical events, and objects of everyday life. Taken together, these paintings form a picture of traditional Cheyenne society not unlike that of a museum display. West has also done some works that look very abstract and nontraditional. A closer look shows that he has used traditional forms and symbols, but in new and imaginative ways.

Dick West, Sr., is also a teacher and lecturer. For more than twenty years at Bacone College, in Muskogee, Oklahoma, he inspired many Indian students to explore their artistic roots with boldness and imagination. As a teacher, he was noted for his deep concern that students understand accurately their cultural heritage when using traditional subjects and designs in their painting. As a lecturer, he sometimes speaks about a series of oil paintings he has done showing Christ as a Plains Indian.

West says that his primary aim has been to show that Indians, with their rich heritage, have an important place in contemporary American art. The goals of Dick West, Sr., in both his art and his teaching, match well his son's goal of creating a great new American museum.

❧ ❧ ❧ ❧

Oscar Howe
Yankton Dakota painter
1915–1983

Oscar Howe felt that American Indian artists should be free to create on their own terms. But during much of the twentieth century, Indians were expected to paint pictures in certain ways that the non-Indian art world recognized as "Indian." Howe, perhaps more than any other American Indian artist, helped break down those restrictive expectations. Through his innovative paintings and vigorous words, he led the way in opening up powerful new stylistic possibilities for younger artists.

Oscar Howe rose above poverty, illness, and prejudice to earn international respect as an artist and teacher. He was born on the Crow Creek Reservation in South Dakota in 1915, in a traditional community of Yankton Dakota (one of the seven divisions of the Dakota nation). His great-grandfather was a tribal recorder who painted symbols on buffalo hides to record events. As a child, Oscar drew too, using charcoal on paper scraps, but his parents discouraged him from this activity, saying that it offered him no future.

Around the age of five or six, Oscar developed a skin disease. The disease caused painful open sores, which looked so bad that other children avoided him. During the long, miserable hours he spent alone, he found comfort in drawing.

When he was seven, Oscar entered one of the worst periods in his life. He was sent to a government-operated Indian boarding school in Pierre, South Dakota. Like many such schools, this school required that students stop speaking their native languages (Oscar didn't know any English). He endured frequent physical punishments for not following school rules. He never had enough to eat, his skin condition worsened, and he developed a painful eye disease. During this time he was away at school his mother died. He was so dreadfully unhappy that at the age of ten he wanted to kill himself. Fortunately for Oscar, the school officials sent him back to the reservation.

After that, things gradually got better. Oscar's health improved, and he grew close to his grandmother. She taught him about the traditional symbols and designs of the Dakota people that would become part of his life's work. Finally, he returned to the school in Pierre, and at the age of eighteen, graduated from eighth grade and found a job as a laborer.

Two years later he was diagnosed with tuberculosis. A warm, dry climate seemed necessary if he was to get well, so he went to New Mexico. There he enrolled at the Santa Fe Indian School, where a famous teacher, Dorothy Dunn, had recently started a program of art instruction. At Santa Fe, Oscar Howe's talent finally blossomed. By the time he graduated from high school in 1938, he had learned much about the basics of art, and he had done paintings that were shown across the United States and in Europe.

Making a living as an artist during the Depression era was very hard. Howe eventually found a job teaching at the Pierre Indian school. The pay was low, but he received commissions to paint the ceiling of the Mitchell Public Library and to paint murals in the city auditorium at Mobridge, both in South Dakota. In 1942, during World War II, Howe was drafted into the U.S. army. He was barely able to complete the second set of paintings in time to report for duty. He served three and a half years, in Europe and North Africa. In Germany, he met his future wife, Heidi Hampel. On returning to South Dakota, Howe won the top award in a prestigious art competition. With the prize money he paid for Heidi's trip to the United States, and the two were married.

Howe's reputation was growing. He became both a college student and artist-in-residence at Dakota Wesleyan University. This arrangement allowed him to earn an income and study at the same time. When he was a senior, he took a temporary leave from being a student in the art department to become the art department chairman. He graduated in 1952, then went on to take a master's degree at the University of Oklahoma. All during the time that he was studying, he exhibited his work and sold paintings nationally.

Howe decided that he would stay in the academic field. For four years he taught in the Pierre public schools. In 1957, he joined the faculty of the University of South Dakota, where he stayed for the rest of his teaching career.

As he gained confidence and maturity as an artist, Howe's painting style changed. When he was at Santa Fe, he, along with all the other students, had

"Origin of the Sioux" by Oscar Howe

been encouraged toward a standard style that involved clear-cut, easily recognizable, often nostalgic images. This "traditional" style was what patrons expected and bought. Although Oscar Howe excelled at this style, he felt it was not a faithful expression of the artistic traditions of his own people, the Dakota. Even if it meant producing works that would not be thought sufficiently "Indian," Howe wanted to remain true to his culture, his people, and himself.

His work began to draw more on design rules from traditional Dakota art. His paintings were brighter in color and felt more active and vital, combining realism and abstraction. They began to look something like European Cubist paintings. In 1958, he submitted one of his newer works to an important Indian art competition where it was rejected as "a fine painting—but not Indian."

Howe's indignant answer set off a chain reaction in the art world. How could his work not be Indian, the full-blooded Yankton wondered. "Are we to be held back forever [to] one phase of Indian painting . . . dictated to, as the Indian always has been?" His pointed arguments influenced artists and patrons alike, and soon many galleries began to fill with paintings by American Indians working in every different style.

"I try to paint the Indian's true identity," Oscar Howe said. By keeping faith with his own maturing artistic vision, Oscar Howe not only broadened the horizons for other artists; he also helped bring all of American art to a new level of maturity.

 за за за за

Pablita Velarde
Santa Clara Pueblo painter
1918–

Pablita Velarde's paintings are dense with the details of her heritage. In one painting, the viewer can see traditional American Indian patterns in the cloth of people's clothing; in another, Velarde depicts the processes used by traditional craftworkers, such as leather tanners and blacksmiths. Another painting shows a ceremonial dance. With care and exactness, her art expresses the traditional Pueblo experience. Perhaps more than any other American Indian woman painter, she has brought the native art of the Southwest to the public eye. She has also created a useful documentary of a way of life that is slipping into the past.

Pablita Velarde's work is rooted in the culture of the Tewa tribe at Santa Clara Pueblo, which is north of Santa Fe, New Mexico. Her parents' families had lived in Santa Clara for many years and valued the traditions of their ancestors. Her grandmother was a medicine woman. At birth, Velarde was given the name Tse-Tsan, meaning "Golden Dawn." Only later in childhood did she receive the name Pablita.

Pablita's family lived in a two-room adobe house near the edge of the pueblo. Religious ceremonies and community activities were held in the pueblo center. Most were related to the seasons, a crucial factor in the life of a farming people in a dry climate. In spring, they held planting ceremonies; in summer, they danced to encourage rain; in fall, they gave thanks for the harvest; in winter, they held contests and feasts. When she was a child, Pablita watched all these activities at the plaza, and they made a vivid impression in her mind.

When Pablita Velarde was about three, she developed an eye disease that made her blind for two years. That time of darkness sharpened her interest in remembering images of Pueblo life. During this time, her father would tell her centuries-old tales about supernatural beings and Pueblo history. These too became part of the mental pictures she formed in her mind.

When she was six, Pablita went to a Catholic mission school in Santa Fe, where she began to learn English and the ways of the world beyond Santa Clara. Beginning with the seventh grade, she attended the Santa Fe Indian School, a government-run boarding school. From then on, painting was the most important interest in her life.

At fourteen, Pablita Velarde began to paint. At the time, students at Indian schools were discouraged from painting Indian subjects. Pablita went ahead anyway and painted the scenes stored in her mind. When she was fifteen and just finished with eighth grade, she did a large oil painting that was shown at the World's Fair in Chicago. About the same time she did several watercolors that were exhibited at the Museum of New Mexico. Compared to her later work, her early paintings were often simple or sketchy or out of proportion, but they were full of artistic promise.

Luckily for Velarde, the school's policy about Indian art was changed. Dorothy Dunn, who later become a famous teacher, was hired as instructor of Indian art, and Pablita was among her first and most outstanding students.

In 1936, after Velarde graduated from the Santa Fe Indian School, she began to teach at a day school in Santa Clara. Then, in 1938, a famous naturalist and lecturer, Ernest Seton Thompson, took an interest in her work, and he asked Pablita to accompany his family on a four-month tour of the United States. The trip gave her a chance to see many new things and to exhibit and sell some of her paintings.

After she returned, Velarde built a small house and studio at Santa Clara (house building was traditionally a women's activity). Some people at the pueblo did not approve of her painting, because painting was traditionally done by men.

"Corn Dance" by Pablita Velarde

The same people had disapproved of her before—they had thought it unnecessary for a woman to complete high school. Velarde's dedication to a career as an artist was making her feel separated from her community, but she persisted with her work. In 1942, she married Herbert Hardin. Although they established a home in Albuquerque and she lived there many years, Pablita always kept a studio at Santa Clara.

During the years from 1939 to 1948, Pablita Velarde was commissioned to do a series of mural paintings for the museum at Bandelier National Monument in New Mexico, the site of ancient cliff and pueblo ruins. The paintings provide a finely detailed, authentic record of the lore and daily life of the Pueblos. They show an artist whose skill, confidence, and artistic scope were growing.

Pablita took on other murals in commercial buildings and did many tempera and watercolor paintings. In 1956, she began to use "earth colors" to make "earth

paintings." She went out into the New Mexico hills to collect just the right colors of rocks, ground them to powder with a *metate* (corn-grinding stone), and mixed them with water and glue. She applied the resulting paints to a board, creating textured pictures. These pictures resembled the work of Pueblos long ago on the walls of *kivas* (ceremonial chambers that are usually round and partly underground).

By 1960, Velarde had renewed her ties with her family at Santa Clara. She wrote and illustrated *Old Father, the Storyteller*, a prize-winning book of traditional stories told by her father.

Pablita Velarde's work has been sought out by individuals and museums across the United States and abroad. She has received many impressive awards. Her daughter, Helen Hardin, became a painter too. Sometimes their works have been exhibited together. While Pablita Velarde's unique and compelling strength as an artist is derived from the past, Helen Hardin has used her cultural identity as a starting point in creating abstract, highly original images that speak to the modern world.

ン ン ン ン

Frederick L. Dockstader
Oneida and Navajo artist,
anthropologist, and author
1919–

Frederick Dockstader is an author and anthropologist by profession and a silversmith by avocation. His life has been largely devoted to practicing and preserving traditional Indian arts, and to sharing the meaning of these arts with the world.

Dockstader was born in Los Angeles, California, of Oneida and Navajo heritage. He spent much of his childhood on Navajo and Hopi reservations in Arizona, where he was first introduced to the traditional arts of weaving and silversmithing.

After leaving the reservation, Dockstader went on to earn B.A. and M.A. degrees at Arizona State College and a Ph.D. at Western Reserve University. He supported himself during these early years as both a teacher and a silversmith, before beginning a long and illustrious career as a museum curator, university professor, and author.

Dockstader's first book evolved from his graduate studies with the Hopi people. *The Kachina and the White Man*, published in 1954, studied the impact of white influence on the Hopi people. This book began his lifelong interest in the effects of European culture upon native cultures.

Dockstader's primary interest, however, is the many and varied forms of American Indian art. His books *Indian Art in North America* (1962), *Indian Art in Middle America* (1964), and *Indian Art in South America* (1967) represent the first comprehensive survey of native arts in the Americas by a single author.

One of Dockstader's most notable accomplishments was during his stint as Director of the Museum of the American Indian, Heye Foundation, in New York City from 1955 to 1975. The museum housed the largest collection of American Indian artifacts in the world. During his tenure, Dockstader completely reorganized the museum's exhibits and public services. His goal was to successfully introduce museum visitors to American Indian culture so that the artifacts would be more meaningful to all viewers.

During this same period, Dockstader was a tireless advocate for the preservation of Indian arts and artifacts. Because of his dedicated interest and experience, in 1955 he was named a Commissioner of the Indian Arts and Crafts Board of the U.S. Department of the Interior. He remained on this board for more than twenty years, serving as Chairman from 1962 to 1967.

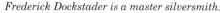

Frederick Dockstader is a master silversmith.

Dockstader has also been awarded innumerable academic honors and served on a variety of councils, academies, and boards. He is highly sought as a lecturer and consultant and has traveled widely throughout the country.

Dockstader is also a practicing silversmith. He is active in the design, working, and teaching of the art, and his prize-winning works have been exhibited in many museums. It has always been important to him to remain a practitioner, as well as a preserver, of American Indian art forms.

One of Dockstader's longstanding interests has been in the area of Navajo weaving. This weaving, once feared to be vanishing, is now thriving as art and business for the Navajos who practice it. Unlike some anthropologists, Dockstader sees this weaving as a living, contemporary art form, subject to change and innovation, and not meant only for museum exhibition. In an article written for *American Craft Magazine*, Dockstader wrote:

> Perhaps the most irksome constraint on the contemporary weaver is the tendency of some individuals to "collect by the calendar," regarding anything made in recent times as inferior to those from bygone days. This attitude is in effect a rejection of the living artist and her background, the implication being that today's Navajo culture is inferior . . . at its best, Navajo weaving is accomplished and in many ways far better made and more suitable to today's living than any done in the past.

It is to both preserving artwork from the past and encouraging artists of today that Frederick Dockstader has dedicated his life. As an artist, an author, and an anthropologist, he has done much to ensure that designs from past and present American Indian artists survive to delight and instruct admirers in the future.

ça ça ça ça

The Codetalkers of World War II

American Indian men and women participated in World War II in impressive numbers, both as draftees and as volunteers. By the war's end, about 25,000 Indians had served in the U.S. armed services, as members of the Army, Navy, Marines, and Coast Guard. Indians fought and died on all the war fronts, but they became best known for their involvement in the war in the Pacific, largely because of the fame of the Codetalkers and Ira Hayes.

The Codetalkers' contributions had to be kept secret until the war was over. This special Marine unit of Navajo, Comanche, and Choctaw speakers used complex native languages as a code and played a vital role in the American effort to push the invading Japanese back across the Pacific. The Codetalkers made it possible for Americans to maintain secrecy in their radio and telephone communications, even in the front lines. The Japanese never figured out the meaning of the mysterious voice sounds they intercepted in their earphones.

The idea of basing coded messages on American Indian languages came from a civilian named Philip Johnston. Johnston, the son of a missionary, had been raised among the Navajo. He knew firsthand how hard the language was to learn and how few outsiders had ever mastered it. At the time, only twenty-eight nonnative speakers, none of them Germans or Japanese, knew the complex language. In February 1942, Johnston took his suggestion to the commanding officer of the Marines. Within a few months the first thirty Navajo recruits fluent in both English and their own language were on their way to final training before their first assignment.

That training included learning radio communications procedures and memorizing a specialized list of military terms. The Indians came up with the list of Navajo expressions, with alternates, for English words and phrases that would often be needed in military messages. For example, on the list they had

Navajo words meaning "sparrow hawk" for "dive bomber," "iron fish" for "submarine," and "our mother" for "America."

By the fall of 1942, the first Codetalkers were shipped out to the battle zones in the Pacific. It was immediately clear to commanders in the field that dispatches could be coded, transmitted, and decoded by Codetalkers twice as fast as had been previously possible with other coding methods. The speed of communications was often of vital importance. In addition, the Codetalkers were outstanding Marines. Sometimes they had to work behind enemy lines, and sometimes they were directly involved in fighting as well as communications duties.

Comanche codetalkers gather together in 1941 at Fort Benning, Georgia, for a group photograph.

Before the war was over, more than four hundred American Indians had served as Codetalkers. Their special duties did not mean they were grouped together; for the most part, Codetalkers worked in teams of two assigned as needed throughout all the combat regiments in the Pacific. Wherever the Marines stormed ashore on Japanese-held islands, the Codetalkers were a familiar sight, hunched over their equipment to establish the lifeline of communications for their units.

After the war, when their role was made public, the Codetalkers quickly entered into popular folklore as heroic figures. War movies made during the post-war period frequently included Codetalkers somewhere in the story. In reality, the Codetalkers, like many other American Indian veterans, often came back to a civilian life of inadequate job opportunities and impoverished reservation conditions. Their wartime successes, however, helped raise the American public's awareness of American Indian contributions.

Ira Hayes
Pima (O'odam) soldier and
World War II hero
1922–1955

February 23, 1945, was the day when Ira Hayes' life changed forever. On the island of Iwo Jima, in the western Pacific, while a fierce battle between U.S. and Japanese troops raged around them, Hayes and five other Marines courageously fought their way to the top of Mt. Suribachi. As they struggled to raise an American flag, a photographer captured the moment on film. That picture became one of the most famous images of World War II, and the men in it became almost instant national heroes.

Ira Hamilton Hayes was a Pima (O'odam) from southern Arizona. His parents were farmers, as Pimas have been for centuries. Before he joined the military, Ira's life was like that of any ordinary Indian boy from a poor family in a small, traditional farming village.

In 1942, shortly after the war began, nineteen-year-old Ira Hayes joined the Marine Corps. He was trained as a paratrooper and was sent to the Pacific front of the war, where he saw action in several battle areas. His service earned him a promotion to the rank of corporal.

By early 1945, U.S. forces were steadily advancing across the Pacific toward Japan with the aim of bringing the war to a close. But the Americans still wanted to establish another air base closer to Japan to launch attacks against the mainland. The island of Iwo Jima was a Japanese stronghold, but American military planners thought it would be the right place for such a base.

In February 1945, the Fifth Marine Division assault troops, including

Hayes, landed on Iwo Jima. For weeks the Japanese defenders strenuously resisted the American invasion. There were thousands of casualties on both sides. Mt. Suribachi, an extinct volcano on the southern part of the island, was the scene of some particularly heavy fighting, but it was eventually taken by the Americans. When Hayes and five other Marines planted the American flag on its heights, Associated Press photographer Joe Rosenthal happened to be there to make his dramatic picture of their bravery.

The photograph was soon distributed in newspapers throughout the United States, and it immediately became a source of popular patriotic inspiration. Suddenly there was a flood of interest in the identity of the figures in the picture. The Marine Corps supplied the names of the six men and brought the three who had survived Iwo Jima, including Hayes, back to the United States. They were acclaimed as national heroes, but most of all Hayes. As an Indian, he symbolized in the public imagination a united war effort, one that brought together for a single good cause all of America's different kinds of people. He seemed to be the perfect advertisement to use in a nationwide patriotic campaign.

So Hayes was sent around the country to appear at rallies selling war bonds. He was sent to patriotic celebrations and Red Cross drives. The Iwo Jima flag-raising was depicted on millions of posters and on a postage stamp issued in 1945. After the war ended, the fame continued. A big bronze statue based on the Iwo Jima photograph was put up in Washington, D.C. Everywhere people wanted to honor the famous Ira Hayes. One way they kept honoring him was with offers of free drinks, which he accepted. More and more often he drank to excess.

Hayes did not want or enjoy his fame. Life as a celebrity confused and irritated him. A shy man, he did not like being part of a public show. He was not prepared to handle all the people who, for their own selfish reasons, swarmed around him. He was troubled by the unfairness of the special treatment he received, because he felt he was no more heroic than many other soldiers. He said he wished "that guy had never made that picture."

The raising of the flag on Iwo Jima

In the years after the war, Hayes was less and less able to make sense of his life. An alcoholic, he drifted uncertainly from job to job, never finding one that worked out well. He was arrested dozens of times for drunkenness, occasions that often began with friendly offers of a congratulatory drink from his admirers.

Several times he tried to speak up publicly about issues that concerned him, especially the government's neglectful treatment of the Pimas. No one seemed to be listening. Only Ira Hayes, the hero and the symbol, caught America's attention. Toward the end of his life, in hopes of sorting his life out with his family's help, he went back to the reservation where he was born. He died there, of alcohol and exposure to the cold on a January night, at the age of thirty-three.

The Echohawks

Brummett Echohawk
Pawnee artist, writer, and actor
1922–

John Echohawk
Pawnee attorney
1945–

Larry Echohawk
Pawnee politician
1948–

The Pawnee scout serving under Major Frank North in the U.S. Cavalry in the 1870s was a quiet man. In fact, his name, Echohawk, was given to him to suggest a silent warrior whose deeds are echoed by others.

"The Trail of Tears" by Brummett Echohawk

Echohawk's grandson, Brummett Echohawk, is a noted American artist and illustrator. He was born in Pawnee, Oklahoma, in 1922, and served in the Army from 1940 to 1945, during World War II. During that time he drew combat sketches that were published in the army's *Yank Magazine* and as a syndicated feature in dozens of newspapers. After the war he studied at the Art Institute of Chicago and the Detroit Art Institute.

In 1959 and 1960, Brummett Echohawk worked with the renowned artist Thomas Hart Benton to create the remarkable mural painting *Independence and the Opening of the West* at the Truman Memorial Library in Independence, Missouri. Another of his most famous paintings, entitled *Trail of Tears*, shows the Cherokee people being driven from their homes in the Southeast during the forced removal period of the 1830s. Brummett Echohawk has also acted in plays and television shows, written for newspapers and magazines, and created the comic strip *Little Chief*, appearing in the *Tulsa World*.

The scout had another grandson, Ernest Echohawk, who became a land surveyor. He left the reservation in Oklahoma and moved to New Mexico. He married Emma Jane Conrad. Together they raised two daughters and four sons.

One of those sons is John Echohawk. He is a lawyer who has been deeply involved with the American Indians rights movement since he graduated from law school in 1970. At that time there were probably only about twenty American Indian lawyers in the entire country. One of the things that John Echohawk learned in law school was how little was known about the laws and rights pertaining to American Indians. "A law doesn't do any good until it is enforced," he said. "So we had to learn the legal process."

As part of that effort, shortly after he graduated from law school he went to work for the Native American Rights Fund (NARF). Since its founding, NARF has worked to enforce the law on behalf of many Indian nations and native groups, often with great success. Most of NARF's work has been based on three basic principles. The first is that Indian nations are separate, sovereign governments and state governments have no jurisdiction over them. The second

John Echohawk

is that the federal government has a legal responsibility to assist federally recognized tribes. And the third is that native people have inherent rights to and responsibilities toward the resources on their lands.

Working from these principles, NARF has made significant progress in restoring the status and powers of native governments; in protecting and promoting their rights, especially in regard to education and religion; and in helping them assert their rights to the land, water, mineral, and fishing resources on their reservations. Since 1977, John Echohawk has been executive director of the organization and has seen NARF become nationally recognized and respected for its success in advancing native interests. "It was simply a question," John Echohawk says, recalling the words of one of his law professors, "of enforcing old promises."

John's brother Larry Echohawk is also winning national attention in the world of public affairs. Larry Echohawk attended college on a football scholarship and then went on to get a law degree. In 1978, be became the principal lawyer for the Shoshone-Bannock tribes of southern Idaho, and in 1982 he was elected to the Idaho House of Representatives. He was only the second American Indian to win election to that body, and he quickly earned a reputation as an effective legislator.

In 1990, he took on his biggest challenge: he decided to run for the post of Idaho's Attorney General. The challenge was great because he is a Democrat in a mostly Republican state, and the campaign against him was highly negative and included racist overtones. Nevertheless, Larry Echohawk won by a margin of 56 to 44 percent. He thus became one of the very few American Indians ever to win a statewide elected position. An unintended result of his victory is that now Larry and John may one day have to face each other on opposite sides in a court dispute involving Indian rights versus a state government's rights.

Another of John and Larry's brothers is also a lawyer. And a sister, Lucille Echohawk, is a financial aid officer for the Council of Energy Resource Tribes, an organization that represents tribes with energy resources on their reservations.

Clearly, the contributions and achievements of this distinguished family have been great and show every promise of influencing a great many people.

Larry Echohawk

Maria Tallchief
Osage ballerina
1925–

Her dancing was an unforgettable combination of dazzling brilliance and flawless elegance. Ballet lovers everywhere were astonished and delighted. More than any other single dancer, Maria Tallchief proved that American ballet dancers could rank among the world's very best. Until she achieved renown, European ballet dancing was traditionally considered superior to American ballet. But Tallchief's stunning performances helped change that idea forever.

The woman that *Newsweek* magazine called "the finest American-born classic ballerina the twentieth century has produced" was born on the Osage reservation in Oklahoma in 1925, in the little town of Fairfax. Maria Tallchief, the daughter of an Osage father and a Scotch-Irish mother, grew up in a rather well-to-do family. Like other Osages, the Tallchiefs shared in the profits from oil that was being pumped from the tribal land. Aside from participating in special ceremonial occasions, the family did not live a very traditional Osage life. But their grandmother, Elizabeth Big Heart, kept their Osage heritage alive by recalling memories of her youth and telling stories of the old ways.

By the time Maria was three years old, Maria's mother realized that her daughter was unusually gifted in music. Hoping that those talents might someday make Maria a concert pianist, Maria's mother arranged for her to take piano lessons and dancing lessons. Maria's younger sister, Marjorie, seemed to have the makings of a fine dancer, so Mrs. Tallchief arranged for her to take lessons, too.

Nearly every day during her childhood Maria practiced piano and dancing for hours, in addition to attending regular school. She was a hard-working, serious student. For a long time she was uncertain if she preferred dancing or playing the piano, but she knew she enjoyed both, and one of them would be her future.

When she was about eight, the Tallchief family moved to Los Angeles so the two daughters could study with the best music and dancing teachers available. By the time she was a teenager, Maria had decided that she wanted to become a dancer rather than a pianist. Her career was launched at the age of fifteen. Maria studied with the legendary Russian ballet teacher Madame Nijinska. Nijinska had created a ballet and selected Tallchief to be the principal soloist at its performance at the Hollywood Bowl.

In 1942, soon after graduating from high school, Tallchief joined a well-known dance company called the Ballet Russe de Monte Carlo. For a while she had to endure many new pressures and frustrations. She had to learn a great deal in a short time, and the dancing was physically demanding. Her natural reserve and seriousness put off the other dancers, and she sometimes felt alone and unhappy. Yet her drive for excellence did not fail, and her dancing was always outstanding.

George Balanchine, the great Russian-born choreographer, took over the direction of the Ballet Russe and soon noticed Tallchief's startling speed, strength, and precision. He began to arrange ballets with her cast in increasingly prominent and difficult roles. She worked tirelessly and her performances were ever more breathtaking. In Balanchine's ballets, Tallchief became a sensational success. She was granted the title of ballerina, an honor the Ballet Russe had never given an American before.

When she was twenty-one, Maria Tallchief married George Balanchine. The next year they both joined the New York City Ballet. Although their marriage lasted only a few years, Maria spent most of the rest of her performing career with the New York City Ballet, where she was best known for more than thirty roles she danced in ballets created for her by Balanchine.

Maria Tallchief in costume for a role at the New York City Ballet

Probably the most famous of these roles was in *The Firebird*. Audiences were amazed at how, as she danced the title role, she seemed magically transformed into a flashing, soaring, flame-creature. Her spectacular performance confirmed her position as prima ballerina of the New York City Ballet and as one of the finest ballerinas in the world.

Many people said that as the years passed her dancing gained a more radiant and poetic quality. She earned acclaim from critics and audiences everywhere. Among the honors that came to her was a special award from the Osages. The tribal council named her Wa-Xthe-Thonba (Woman of Two Standards) in recognition of her importance in two worlds—the Osage world and the world of other cultures.

In 1966, at the age of forty and after a career of a quarter century, Maria Tallchief announced her retirement. She had been married to a Chicago businessman for nearly a decade, so she moved to that city to become a director and teacher with two ballet companies. Still involved in the world of dance, she is now also active in various Chicago civic organizations.

Maria Tallchief is remembered for her thrilling performances and for the respect she brought to American ballet. Her television appearances inspired thousands of American girls to pursue their dream of becoming ballerinas.

While she was the most well-known of American Indian ballerinas, Maria Tallchief was only one of five American Indian women from Oklahoma who became world-class ballerinas around the same time. Another of this group was Maria's sister, Marjorie Tallchief, who had a very distinguished career as a dancer, mainly in Europe. Yvonne Chouteau, a Cherokee; Rosella Hightower, a Choctaw; and Moscelyne Larkin, a Shawnee, also were remarkable artists who became very well known in the 1940s and 1950s.

The contributions of these five dancers have been recognized by the state of Oklahoma with ceremonies and celebrations. In 1982, a large bronze sculpture honoring them was unveiled in Tulsa near the Performing Arts Center as part of the diamond jubilee commemoration of Oklahoma statehood. In 1992, a

The five American Indian ballerinas gather at the Oklahoma State Capitol for the dedication of a mural by Mike Larken in their honor. From left, Yvonne Choureau, Rosella Hightower, Maria Tallchief, Margorie Tallchief, and Moscelyne Larkin.

painting of the five ballerinas was commissioned by the State Arts Council of Oklahoma for the Oklahoma State Capitol. All five attended the dedication. It was the first time they had all been together at the same time.

Louis Ballard

Quapaw and Cherokee composer
1931–

When Louis Ballard was a young music student, he came across many musical compositions that were supposed to capture the sound of American Indian music. Yet he knew from his own experience that much of this music was based on musical stereotypes that lacked any real Indian essence. A challenge began to form in his mind: the idea of creating music that combined a true Indian musical expression with elements of modern Western music that would appeal to audiences. Since that time, he has devoted his career to this goal, and to teaching young Indians who want to learn about and carry forward their own musical heritages.

Louis Ballard was born in a farming family in the northeast corner of Oklahoma in 1931, in a place called Devil's Promenade. On his mother's side he was Quapaw, and on his father's side Cherokee. Louis' childhood was a mix of happy and unhappy times. Living with his grandmother in her house on Quapaw tribal land, he felt comfortable and free. But when he was with his mother and stepfather, who lived in a white community, he often felt belittled and excluded. He was miserable when he was sent to a government-operated boarding school, where young Indians were expected to break all ties with their tribal cultures. Learning to live in both the reservation and the larger society was difficult and confusing.

Amid such uncertainties Louis found increasingly that music meant a great deal to him. His mother, who played the piano and wrote children's songs, introduced him to traditional Quapaw music. Louis began playing and writing his own songs at an early age, and as he grew he developed a strong interest in the music and traditional culture of other tribes as well. It seemed that music allowed him to touch something enduring and important, and through music he could express his understanding of the different worlds he had experienced.

At the University of Oklahoma and the University of Tulsa, Louis Ballard received a broad musical training that emphasized piano and composing. Later he took private lessons with several famous teachers of composition, and he continued collecting and studying the music of many tribal groups. The more he learned, the more fascinated he became with the idea of blending Indian music into the American musical mainstream.

In his compositions, Ballard has used a variety of musical forms. He has written works for full orchestra, ballets, music for solo performers, small groups, and chorus. He frequently includes instruments and rhythms that are new to his audiences. In part of the woodwind quintet *Ritmo Indio*, for example, the usual oboe is replaced by a *wi-iki-zho*, a flutelike instrument used by the Lakota in courtship rituals. More than forty traditional Indian instruments are needed for *Cacega Ayuwipi* (*The Decorative Drum*), a percussion piece.

Often he is inspired by traditional lore or by history. One of Ballard's best known works is *Koshare*, a ballet that draws on the Hopi story of the creation of the world and the evolution of people. *The Four Moons* is another ballet first danced in 1967 in commemoration of Oklahoma's sixtieth anniversary as a state. It concerns the coming together in Oklahoma of four tribes, the Cherokee, Shawnee, Choctaw, and Osage, after long forced migrations from their ancient homelands. For this Ballard not only wrote the score, but also designed the costumes and stage sets as well. *Incident at Wounded Knee* is a remembrance of the 1890 slaughter of Oglala Sioux at Wounded Knee, South Dakota, and also the bitter conflict there in 1973.

In addition to creating numerous musical compositions, Louis Ballard has been very busy as a teacher, especially of Indian young people. During his career, he has taught in Oklahoma public schools, written textbooks, headed the Music and Performing Arts departments at the Institute of American Indian Arts, and served as the national director in charge of music education programs in all federal Indian schools, among other activities. His composing and teaching have earned him a long list of prestigious awards and honors. As a teacher, Ballard stresses to his students that they should learn the authentic performing style for the tribal music they study, including such details as proper pronunciation of sounds and words. They should also learn about the cultural setting from which the music emerges. He feels that students participating in tribal music as it was meant to be played have the opportunity to make direct contact with their history. Through that experience they can discover the beauty and complexity of their cultural heritage.

"Portrait of Will Rogers" by Louis Ballard, a vocal and a choral musical composition

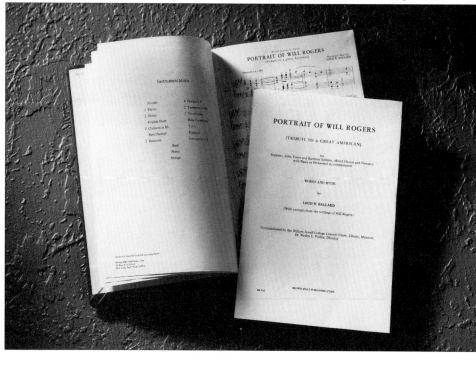

LaDonna Harris

Comanche president of Americans
for Indian Opportunity

1931–

When LaDonna Harris was growing up in Cotton County, Oklahoma, she rode horses bareback, floated on logs in the creek, and in the evening did chores such as gathering eggs and watering plants on the family farm. Today, she moves with ease and energy in a very different world. She is a high-powered activist in Washington, D.C., the head of an national organization that provides Indian tribal governments with information and assistance and promotes economic self-sufficiency.

LaDonna Harris is a Comanche, and she values that heritage very much. When she was a child, she felt related to everyone in the Comanche tribe. Her family and community gave her a wonderful sense of who she was and where she belonged. She feels that this experience of belonging is the reason she so actively pursues it for others today.

LaDonna was raised by her grandparents in a traditional Comanche environment. Her grandparents spoke only the Comanche language at home, and they dressed in traditional clothes. Her grandfather, Tabbytite, was a successful farmer and cattleman. He was also an Eagle medicine man, and she remembers being healed by him when she was sick. When he was young, Tabbytite was sent to a government boarding school. He often told LaDonna about how the school authorities tried to make him give up his Comanche ways, and how he ran away from school when they tried to cut off his long black braids.

When she started school, LaDonna felt discriminated against because she was Indian. She was embarrassed and confused by the jeers and insults of some of the children on the bus she rode every day. Although it was a painful experience, she feels she was able to handle difficult situations only because her family and other Indian people had given her enough inner strength.

In high school, LaDonna met Fred Harris, the son of a poor white sharecropper. Shortly after he entered college they were married. From the beginning, their marriage was very much a sharing partnership. During their early years together, they had very little money, and they had to struggle to pay for Fred's education through college and law school while bringing up three children. Their hard work paid off, however. Fred had a career in public service. In 1964, he was elected to the first of two terms as U.S. Senator from Oklahoma.

LaDonna Harris, president of the AIO, regularly meets with tribal leaders around the country to help them achieve goals they have set for themselves.

Later he was candidate for president of the United States. LaDonna, meanwhile, was increasingly involved in issues closest to her heart: Indian rights, economic opportunity, and education. Tough, smart, and outspoken in her opinions, she became a highly effective advocate for the issues she cared so passionately about.

LaDonna was actively involved in Fred's campaigns for political office. She became the first wife of a congressional member to testify before Congress. In 1965, she was a principal organizer of a statewide meeting of Indians in Oklahoma who gathered together to discuss problems in their communities and to share information about possible solutions. Out of that conference grew an organization called Oklahomans for Indian Opportunity, with LaDonna Harris as president.

Five years later, she founded a similar national organization, Americans for Indian Opportunity (AIO), which she still heads today. AIO assists tribes in achieving a variety of goals that they set for themselves. AIO helps tribes in areas such as preserving the environmental quality in a region, making appropriate use of natural resources, and setting up health-care systems for people in rural areas.

LaDonna and Fred Harris have three children. Their daughter Catherine Tijarina is president of the Institute of American Indian Arts in Santa Fe, New Mexico. Their other daughter, Laura Harris, is on the staff of the National Museum of the American Indian in Washington, D.C. Byron Harris, their son, works in television production in Los Angeles, California.

In addition to leading AIO for the past two decades, LaDonna Harris has been part of numerous other activities on behalf of American Indians, civil rights, women's rights, and other causes in support of less privileged members of American society. All of her activities reflect the lessons of her life experiences. She has said, "I have learned that the more privileged you are, the more you have to give back. The best contribution I hope I have made is to have helped others to move to another place in their lives."

N. Scott Momaday
Kiowa writer and artist
1934–

O ne of the most distinguished American Indian writers today is N. Scott Momaday. His work, which first appeared in the 1960s, was at the forefront of an exceptional period of Indian literary renewal that continues to the present. His first novel, *House Made of Dawn*, earned him one of the nation's most prestigious awards for literature, the Pulitzer Prize. In addition to being a much-admired novelist, poet, essayist and autobiographer, Momaday has also established a reputation as a fine painter.

Momaday was born in Lawton, Oklahoma, in 1934. When he was a child, his father, a Kiowa artist and teacher, and his mother, a writer and teacher of Cherokee ancestry, accepted jobs in the Southwest. The family lived in Arizona and New Mexico, where Scott spent much of his youth. His parents successfully bridged the gap between the white and Indian worlds. They encouraged their son to appreciate the various Indian cultures around him, and also to feel at home in the white world.

As a child, Scott often returned to Oklahoma for visits with his grandparents. There he came to know his Kiowa heritage. He listened to and watched with fascination as his grandparents and other elderly Kiowas related stories of his family and tribal past. Later he wrote that the aged Kiowa visitors to his grandparents' home "were made of lean and leather" and "wound their braids with strips of colored cloth. . . . They were an old council of warlords come to remind and be reminded of who they were." Momaday's grandmother had attended the last Kiowa Sun Dance ceremony in 1887. From her, he learned stories about their Kiowa ancestors, making her memories his own.

Except for one year of high school at a military academy in Virginia, Momaday attended schools on the Indian reservations where his parents taught and in Santa Fe and Albuquerque, New Mexico. Then he went on to the University of New Mexico, where he earned a bachelor's degree in political science in 1958. Following college, he taught school on a reservation for a year. During this period, he began seriously exploring his interest in writing creatively.

Momaday decided to study literature and entered Stanford University's graduate school in California. At Stanford, Momaday was an outstanding student, winning several fellowships and awards. As Momaday developed as a writer, he merged elements together from his various cultural backgrounds.

After he received his Ph.D. in 1963, Momaday began to teach English and literature. Through the years, he has been a professor at the University of California, Stanford University, and the University of Arizona.

Momaday's *House Made of Dawn*, published in 1968, was the book that made him famous and won him the Pulitzer Prize. It received more acclaim than any previous novel by an American Indian, and it paved the way for other writers. *House Made of Dawn* is about the struggles of a part-Indian veteran of World War II as he tries to adjust to civilian life and to find his personal identity. Eventually he finds healing and order through tribal traditions.

The next year Momaday's *The Way to Rainy Mountain* was published. It is one of several autobiographical works he has produced. It recounts traditional stories of three hundred years of journeys of the Kiowa people ending at Rainy Mountain in Oklahoma, together with family and tribal history as well as his own recollections. The result is a poetic and imaginative tour of the influences that shaped him. As Momaday has said, "The imaginative experience and the historical express equally man's reality."

For Momaday, the places that people experience are important, because places help determine the kind of people we become. Momaday's writing reveals a vivid, finely tuned sense of landscapes. In *The Way to Rainy Mountain*, Momaday talks about how necessary it is to understand thoroughly and truly the places we have known:

> Once in his life a man ought to concentrate his mind upon the remembered earth, I believe. He ought to give himself up to a particular landscape in his experience, to look at it from as many angles as he can, to wonder about it, to dwell upon it. He ought to imagine that he touches it with his hands at every season and listens to the sounds that are made upon it. He ought to imagine the creatures there and all the faintest motions of the wind. He ought to recollect the glare of noon and all the colors of the dawn and dusk.

A traditional Kiowa scene of a young boy breaking a pony

The Names, published in 1976, is another autobiographical work. Returning to the theme that people are molded by the places in their experience, Momaday describes the history of both sides of his family and his own childhood and youth. Both *The Way to Rainy Mountain* and *The Names* are written in a clear style like that of traditional Indian storytellers.

In addition to many essays, short articles, and several other books of prose, Momaday has written two volumes of poetry. And following in the steps of his father, he is a painter as well. Although he did not exhibit his paintings until 1979 when he was well established in his writing career, he has since had shows in the United States and in Europe.

಄ ಄ ಄ ಄

Billy Mills
Oglala Lakota Olympic athlete
1938–

At the 1964 Olympic games in Tokyo, an unknown American distance runner, an Oglala Lakota named Billy Mills, set a world's record in the 10,000-meter race. It was a spectacular upset — one of the most memorable victories in the history of international athletic competition.

Television cameras followed thirty-six of the world's best runners as they competed for the gold. Just as the runners neared the homestretch, one accidentally bumped into Billy Mills, causing him to fall back. In an incredible recovery, Billy pulled back up and then ahead of the others to win. Setting a new record time, Billy Mills became the first and only American to win an Olympic gold medal in this event. The drive and determination that made him a champion in 1964 are still with him today, channeled into other activities. Billy Mills travels to Indian communities across the country to inspire young people and encourage physical fitness, pride, and self-reliance. He has learned from his own experiences about the need for such messages.

Billy Mills was born on the Pine Ridge Reservation in South Dakota. He and his seven brothers and sisters were orphaned when he was twelve. Left without much money, Billy was sent away to a government boarding school for Indians. He attended high school at the Haskell Institute in Kansas, where he discovered running. Because of his athletic abilities, he won a full scholarship to the University of Kansas.

After graduating with a degree in education, Mills joined the Marines. For a while, he didn't give much thought to competitive running. However, when people began encouraging him to run, he began to train seriously. He qualified for the Olympic trials, and from there ran to his astonishing victory in Tokyo.

Billy was admired by young American Indians. The Lakota honored him with ceremonies and gifts, including a special ring made of gold from the Black Hills—an area that the Lakota, Dakota, and Cheyenne hold sacred. He still wears the ring. Billy recalls that when he received the ring, a Lakota chief reminded him that with his achievement and good fortune came a responsibility to give back something in return. Since then, he has tried to meet that responsibility.

Billy Mills breaks an Olympic record at the 1964 Summer Olympics in Tokyo.

Billy continued to run competitively for several years after Tokyo, and he set other track records. But when the team for the next Olympic games was selected, injuries and disagreements about his eligibility edged him out of a slot. Although the spotlight of publicity was fading, Billy Mills was still in demand for public appearances. Besides making public appearances, however, Billy also was establishing himself in the insurance business. He briefly took a job with the Bureau of Indian Affairs, speaking to Indian students in government schools, but decided that he could be more effective on his own. As his athletic career wound down, he focused more on his insurance business and being an independent advocate for Indian interests and physical fitness.

Billy is now president of Billy Mills Enterprises, a thriving California insurance and public relations firm. In the course of his speaking activities over the years, he has visited nearly every reservation and urban Indian community in the country. He listens to people and shares lessons he has learned in his own life. His talks are meant to support and inspire people and encourage them to pursue better opportunities in their lives. Physical fitness, as a means of understanding oneself, is a central theme in all of his speeches.

In 1983, Billy's story was made into an award-winning movie, *Running Brave*. Billy thinks of it as a small part of what he can give in return for the opportunities he was given on the road to his success.

George Abrams
Seneca anthropologist and museum director
1939–

"We have to present a positive picture of all that has been, will be, and can be for the American Indian people." That is the goal that George Abrams sees for his work in museums. He says his real job has always been that of an educator, passing on to the future a great store of knowledge and all the possibilities that knowledge contains. He feels that museums must be useful, vital, up-to-date centers of learning that help all people understand the richness and diversity of native cultures. Directing a museum is like sharing resources in a large extended family, he feels.

Most recently George Abrams has worked in New York City at the Museum of the American Indian, now part of the new National Museum of the American Indian. But before coming to New York City, he was with the Seneca-Iroquois National Museum, close to his birthplace, in Salamanca, New York, on the Allegany Indian Reservation. At that museum he was in a very real sense sharing resources with his extended family.

Abrams is a member of the Seneca Nation of Indians, and a member of the Heron clan. His Seneca name is Ha-doh-jus, which means "grown up." He was the youngest of five children in a family that generally kept to traditional Seneca ways. The family lived in a rural environment on the reservation.

When he was five, George started to go to a school on the reservation where there were both Indian and white children. At first he hated it; it was a strange and uncomfortable new experience and he ran away. But he went back and attended the school until about the time he entered third grade, when the family moved about sixty miles away to Buffalo, New York. He continued to live in Buffalo until he was in graduate school, making frequent trips back to his old home on the reservation. Even now he still maintains strong ties to his first home.

When he was very young, before he had ever heard the word "anthropologist," George was eager to learn more about why people behaved and lived the way they did. He observed that traditional-minded Indian people were in some ways different from other people. He wondered why, for example, they conducted certain ceremonies in particular ways. Around the age of eight or nine, he discovered that anthropology is the study of human culture and behavior, things that had already begun to excite his interest and curiosity. He stayed fascinated with anthropology, studying it through college, a master's degree, and a Ph.D. program, eventually deciding to apply his interest to museum work.

The National Museum of the American Indian is the home of one of the world's largest and finest collections of objects, photographs, and books associated with native peoples of North, Central, and South America. George Gustav Heye, the son of a wealthy oilman, spent roughly the first half of this century gathering most of the artifacts, or handmade objects, that now make up the core of the museum's collection. Heye was not always selective about what he

Exhibits at the National Museum of the American Indian in New York City

collected. There are stories that he sometimes arrived in a limousine at an Indian reservation and bought everything that he possibly could. The result of his collecting was an astonishing variety and quantity of materials that were in fact sometimes too much to take care of properly.

The best museums are not dusty, jumbled storerooms of artifacts visited only by scholars. Anthropological museums today are building new relationships to the living cultures that have contributed their artifacts. More and more, museums are striving to educate the public about the present-day realities of native cultures and to respond to the concerns and interests of native peoples.

Some of the most difficult issues that museums face are about what to do with the sacred objects and human remains in their collections. Many of these items were stolen or otherwise removed from where they belonged in the past. Museums must ask whether it is responsible and respectful to keep them. Some such items are being reclaimed by tribes and returned to their care. In deciding what to do, museums must balance the sometimes conflicting needs and wishes of tribal people, scholars, and the museum-going public. While George Abrams was at the National Museum of the American Indian, a federal law was passed that affects the decision-making policy regarding sacred objects in museum collections. The change has been hailed by many American Indians who see it as a breakthrough in recognizing and respecting Indian religion and culture as a vital aspect of society today.

Too often the dominant culture in America has ignored contemporary native peoples, treating them as if their traditions and cultures no longer existed. Museums have a special opportunity and obligation to correct this misunderstanding. With leaders such as George Abrams working to devise new responses to this challenge museums, will succeed.

George Abrams has been a professor at the university level and served with many organizations concerned with museums and Indians. For most of his life in one way or another, he has provided people with the opportunity to learn.

Simon Ortiz
Acoma Pueblo writer
1941–

In American Indian cultures, most of the thoughts and words that have been handed down from the distant past have come in oral form. But the oral tradition is more than a way of preserving a great treasury of ceremonies, stories, and songs from other times. It is also a part of a harmonious, balanced life in the present. When old stories are retold and old songs sung again, the storyteller or singer can overlap old and new elements, recombining and adapting them to fit the needs of the living moment.

The poems and stories of Simon Ortiz are rooted in the oral tradition of the Acoma Pueblo people. Ortiz grew up in a small village in the Acoma Pueblo homeland in the 1940s, near Albuquerque, New Mexico. His first language, Keresan—the language of his ancestors—awakened his love of the spoken word and inspired him to become a writer. Ortiz sees language as an almost magical thing at the very center of human existence: "it is language that brings us into being in order to know life." Language is the tool that people use to see and understand themselves, and then to continue being themselves.

Both of Ortiz's parents were storytellers and singers of traditional songs. His family was poor. They got by on a combination of his father's railroad job and subsistence farming. But even as a child Simon knew that there was wealth and strength to be found in his people's cultural heritage. Through the stories and songs of his parents and others, he developed a deep connection with his community, both the people and the place. Ortiz remembers that often after dinner his father would get out his drum and sing as the children danced to narratives about important themes, such as rain, land, hunting, and people. He also recalls hearing the words of his elderly grandfather, who represented a special link with many past generations of grandfathers and grandmothers.

From his family Ortiz also absorbed an intense interest in acquiring knowledge, first by listening to people in the community, and later in school. He attended day school in his village through the sixth grade, and then went to Indian boarding schools in Santa Fe and Albuquerque. Fortunately, his teachers recognized his love of language and encouraged it. He went on to college, left to spend three years in the army, and returned to complete both a bachelor's degree and a master's degree in writing.

Ortiz wrote his first published poem, a Mother's Day poem, in fifth grade. As a teenager he did a great deal of writing. When he was away from home at school, he found that keeping a diary helped him feel less lonely and homesick. But even though language, storytelling, and writing were very important to Simon, it was not until he was in his twenties that he was sure he wanted a career as a writer.

His topics and themes have never been far from the experience of being an Indian. Ortiz often expresses what he calls the "fight-back" of native peoples, who must struggle against the forces in American civilization that threaten their existence. While his writing is especially concerned with the past and the present-day situation of the Acoma Pueblo people, his concerns really extend to all of American society.

Ortiz's writing is clear, natural, direct, and flowing, reflecting a lifetime's interest in language and ideas. He often writes of ordinary, everyday things— taking a trip, seeing children grow up, making stew—and quietly reveals a larger meaning or importance in them. Sometimes he weaves Indian history, philosophy, and symbols into his stories and poems. Many of his stories involve Coyote, a changeable being that appears in different forms in many traditional stories of various tribes.

Some of Ortiz' stories and poems have highlighted the destructive side of the relationship between Indians and non-Indians, or between human beings and the rest of the natural world.

Acoma Pueblo

Yet a current of optimism seems to run through all his writing—a profound hope that both people and nature will survive to continue all the cycles of life and that

> The future will not be mad with loss and waste though
> the memory will be there; eyes will become kind
> and deep, and the bones of this nation will mend. . . .

Simon Ortiz, like many other American Indians, has found continuity and renewal in his cultural heritage. In "It Doesn't End, Of Course," he describes its ageless inspiration:

> It doesn't end.
>
> In all growing
> from all earths
> to all skies,
>
> in all touching
> all things,
>
> in all soothing
> the aches of all years,
>
> it doesn't end.

❧ ❧ ❧ ❧

Tribal Termination and Self-Determination

In the years following World War II, U.S. government policies toward American Indians gradually changed. Previous policy, established by the Indian Reorganization Act of 1934, supported traditional Indian culture and encouraged greater Indian control over tribal affairs. But fifteen years later, legislators were ready to reverse that policy.

For one thing, old notions about Indians were coming back. People were saying, in effect, "make Indians stop being different and separate from the rest of America, and soon they will be absorbed into the general population." There were other people who were convinced that a change in Indian policy was desirable because it would reduce government spending and save taxpayers' money. In the 1950s these ideas came together in a government plan called "termination."

The termination plan called for the federal government to end its financial obligations and compensations to Indian nations, which were stipulated in previous agreements and treaties. According to the termination plan, federal officials would decide which tribes could be severed from the federal relationship. The "terminated" tribes would then assume payments for services such as health care and education, which were, according to previous treaties, obligations of the U.S. government. Indians would have to rely on tribal and state governments to provide services and would be taxed to pay for public institutions such as schools and hospitals. Advocates of termination expected that such changes would force Indians to become assimilated into the American mainstream and the "Indian problem" would be solved.

During the mid-1950s Congress passed several termination laws. But within a few years, it was clear that the plan was a bad one. Many Indian nations were shocked to find themselves severed from the federal relationship and on a fast slide into poverty.

The Menominee tribe, one of the first to be terminated, provides an example of the disasters caused by the termination policy. Federal officials considered the Menominee people living in northeastern Wisconsin ready for termination. In 1951, the tribe received millions of dollars in settlement of lawsuits against the federal government. In addition, the reservation had a lumber mill and a valuable stand of timber. Government officials, however, did not consider the fact that very few Indians understood the meaning of the termination policy for the Menominee people.

Menominee and students at the
University of Wisconsin march on Madison to publicize their message for justice.

Menominee termination took effect in 1961. The tribal government had decided to make the reservation into a county of Wisconsin. It had also created a corporation, made up of all the tribal members, to own and manage all the tribe's assets. The corporation was called Menominee Enterprises, Inc. (MEI). Of course, soon after termination, MEI, as the tribe's only property owner, had to begin paying state and federal taxes. So MEI went to tribal members to raise the money.

The Menominee people, unable to meet state and federal taxes, often had to sell their homes and farms and go on welfare. As a result, much of the land got into the hands of real estate developers, who began slicing up some of the best property into lots for sale to outsiders. The reservation hospital and schools did not have enough money to continue operating, and they closed down. Within a few years the health of many people had deteriorated badly. Meanwhile, the sawmill installed new equipment that required fewer employees, and many Menominees lost their jobs.

Termination was a political failure, too. The government wound up with big expenses for unemployment compensation and welfare payments, rather than the intended savings. And Menominees found their individual freedoms limited by various new restrictions imposed by state laws and MEI.

Activists among the Menominee people managed to turn the situation around. In the late 1960s, a group called DRUMS (Determination of Rights and Unity for Menominee Shareholders) campaigned to draw attention to the tribe's problems. They held meetings and picketed real estate offices to try to halt land sales. They enlisted the help of other Indian nations and organizations and lobbied members of the Congress. By 1975, their efforts had paid off. The termination policy was fully reversed for the Menominees, and they were restored to their old status as a tribe with a reservation.

In all, only about three percent of Indians across the United States were in terminated groups, and only about three percent of Indian land was affected by termination. But the psychological impact of the policy was devastating. The policy of termination was so hated that it became a rallying point for the growing activism among American Indians. By the mid-1960s, there were numerous organizations, driven in part by anger over termination, working to gain greater Indian control over Indian affairs.

During President Richard Nixon's administration in the early 1970s, the federal government once again revised Indian policy. The name for the new approach was "self-determination." At different times, the concept of self-determination was interpreted somewhat differently. The basic intent, however, was to respect the right of Indian people to retain their tribal values, culture, and their own sense of community. They would not have to fend off others who were trying to take their land or who were pushing them to merge with the dominant society. The federal government's responsibilities and special relationships with tribes would be maintained until the Indians themselves chose otherwise.

Self-determination was the principle behind a variety of laws and government programs. These laws and programs centered around self-government and economic development issues. Some made substantial funds available and gave tribes a major voice in deciding how the money would be spent. The laws concerned, among other things, aid for Indian education, preserving and developing tribal assets and natural resources, settling Indian land claims, restoring tribal governments, preventing adoption of Indian children outside the tribe, and raising basic living standards on Indian reservations. Perhaps the most important of these laws was the Indian Self-Determination and Education Act of 1975, which gave tribes increased powers over education and health programs.

Many people said that more far-reaching plans than self-determination were needed to correct the long-standing problems of poverty and despair on most Indian reservations. Many observers, especially non-Indians, were bothered by the way that tribal leaders handled the financial and administrative responsibilities that self-determination laws gave them. They expected Indian leaders to show immediate expertise in self-government without considering the fact that it was entangled in a massive body of state and federal laws. Thus, self-determination did not solve the fundamental problem of the special status of Indians—the built-in tension between the government's role as trustee for tribes and the Indian need to achieve self-sufficiency.

During the 1980s and 1990s, government policy officially remained much the same. In keeping with the pro-business spirit of recent times, the focus has been on economic self-development of tribes even though most tribes occupy unproductive, isolated reservations and have little business expertise. But this has also been an era of budget-cutting in government. In spite of existing treaty obligations, far less money has been spent on programs benefitting Indians. Faced with mounting unemployment and lack of government support, a few Indian nations achieved prosperity by establishing highly successful tribal businesses.

In this period, courtrooms have been the site of some of the most important changes advancing American Indian rights and interests. A new generation of young Indian lawyers, such as those working with the Native American Rights Fund, has been untangling several hundred years' worth of complex laws and treaties pertaining to Indians. They are proving very effective at winning legal decisions that favor Indian people. For the foreseeable future, the best hope for real Indian self-determination may lie not in a broad national policy, but in finding ways to uphold legal agreements that already exist.

ॐ ॐ ॐ ॐ

Buffy Sainte-Marie
Cree musician, songwriter, and activist
1942–

She is a singer and composer whose music, she says, "comes from the soles of my feet." She is also a writer, a lecturer, and a tireless activist for American Indian rights. Committed to both her musical gift and her Indian heritage, she wants people everywhere "to come and hear triumphant music that underlines the joy, beauty, and dignity of being Indian." All around the world, fans of Buffy Sainte-Marie are happy to do just that.

Beverly Sainte-Marie was born on the Piapot Indian Reservation at Craven, Saskatchewan, Canada, on February 20, 1942. Her parents—both Cree Indians—died when she was only a few months old, and she was adopted by Albert and Winifred Sainte-Marie. The Sainte-Maries, who were part Micmac, brought Buffy, as she was soon nicknamed, to the United States, where she grew up in Massachusetts and Maine.

Buffy was a shy and solitary child whose favorite pastime was daydreaming. She spent hours wandering in the woods near her home, writing poems and making up simple tunes. At four, she taught herself to play; at seventeen she was given her first, much longed-for, guitar.

After Buffy graduated from high school, she attended the University of Massachusetts where she soon became a popular campus folk singer. Majoring in Oriental philosophy and education, she was named one of the ten outstanding seniors in her graduating class.

Buffy had always planned to teach after college, but considered a singing career instead. She visited New York City in 1963, where her success at such folk-singing clubs as the Gaslight Cafe, the Bitter End, and Gerde's Folk City convinced her that her decision to become a singer was a good one. She signed with an agent, and was soon appearing in coffee houses, nightclubs, and concerts, and producing a series of best-selling albums. By 1967, she had become a national and international star, appearing at Carnegie Hall and Lincoln Center in New York, the Newport Folk Festival, the Royal Albert Hall in London, Montreal's Expo 67, the Helsinki Music Festival, and on various other music stages in Canada, Mexico, and Europe.

Buffy Sainte-Marie records a song for one of her many albums.

In concert, Buffy is an arresting figure. Her voice is clear and rich, her delivery dramatic. She usually accompanies herself on guitar, or with an American Indian instrument called a mouthbow, which is one of the oldest musical instruments in the world. Buffy's repertoire has always included traditional folk songs as well as material written by contemporary composers. Mostly, though, she has sung the songs she's written herself—more than 200 love ballads, country tunes, city blues, and songs of protest. It is with her protest songs that Buffy Sainte-Marie is most often identified. Committed to the fight for Indian rights and to the antiwar protest movement of the 1960s, Buffy has always used her music to draw attention to problems that need solving.

Still, Buffy insists that she is not primarily a protest singer. As she once told a reporter, "I believe in leaving the politics to the experts—only sometimes the experts don't know what's going on." It was feelings like this that prompted the passionate "Universal Soldier," which became an anthem for the Vietnam war protesters of the 1960s, and the equally impressive "Now That the Buffalo's Gone" and "My Country 'Tis of Thy People You're Dying," which deal with the plight of the American Indian in white America.

Buffy works in many ways to educate people about Indian history and culture, and to improve living conditions of American Indians. She has traveled all over the world, lecturing about past and present American Indian issues. She has visited and lived on Indian reserrvations, and she has written books and articles, produced radio broadcasts, lobbied Washington, and served on a number of advisory councils. In her *Buffy Sainte-Marie Songbook* she writes, "It seems like 90% of my time is spent in court or with the press, trying to explain and remedy the dire problems which cause the Indian suicide rate to be the highest in the country, infant mortality, unemployment, and poverty to be ten and twenty times anybody else's. I am one of the many who are in this to the death. . . ."

In the mid-1970s, Buffy was a regular on the children's television show, *Sesame Street*, even appearing with her infant son, Dakota Starblanket, to teach the show's 8 million young viewers something about her own Cree culture and to show that "Indians say more than 'ugh' and 'how.'" This wasn't Buffy's first time on television—when she appeared in an Indian role in the series *The Virginian* in 1968, she insisted that all the other Indian roles be filled by real Indians as well. It was one of the first times that this type of authenticity was achieved on television.

Buffy Sainte-Marie's legacy extends beyond her singing and writing and lecturing. She established the Nihewan Foundation to channel a percentage of her concert earnings into a non-profit scholarship fund for young American Indians. Throughout her life, Buffy Sainte-Marie has worked hard in both word and deed to plant the "Seeds of Brotherhood" of which she sings in one of her songs. It is her pride in her birthright that leads her to say, "We Indians can dance all the colors of the rainbow . . . I sing the songs of both our summer and our winter."

ès ès ès ès

Will Sampson
Muscogee (Creek) actor
and painter
1934–1987

At a time when most American Indian roles on television and in the movies were played by white actors covered with brown body paint, Will Sampson stood out as someone who was real. With his imposing 6-foot-7-inch frame and his uncompromising integrity, Sampson insisted on playing Indians as real people—not as some hackneyed collection of Hollywood cliches. Sampson's refusal to play to stereotype and his insistence on cultural accuracy heralded a movement toward using American Indian actors on screen and stage.

Will Sampson was a Muscogee (Creek) Indian, born in Okmulgee, Oklahoma, in 1934. Okmulgee has been the center of the Creek tribe since the middle 1800s when the U.S. government forced the Creeks to leave their homelands in Georgia and Alabama for the arid Indian Territory of eastern Oklahoma. The Muscogee in Oklahoma faced the same problems as other American Indian peoples. Many were poor and had no jobs. Their schools were inadequate, and the government offered little assistance. At the time of Will Sampson's birth in 1934, Oklahoma and the nation as a whole were pulling themselves out of a terrible economic Depression. When Will was fourteen, there were few opportunities for an Indian boy in post-dustbowl Oklahoma, so Will turned to rodeo bull riding. As he once told a reporter for the *New York Times*, "When you're an Indian at 14, you have a lot of anger, and [rodeoing is] a way to dispel a lot of it."

Throughout the next twenty-five years, Will Sampson was to try his hand at a lot of different occupations. He knew he had artistic talent, and he drew and painted whenever he could. But painting didn't always pay the bills. To support his growing family (by 1976 he had six children, ranging in age from one to nineteen), he worked as an oil field roughneck, construction worker, linesman, and rodeo rider.

In 1975, Sampson got his first big acting break. A friend suggested he audition for the role of Chief Bromden in the movie adaptation of Ken Kesey's novel *One Flew Over the Cuckoo's Nest*. Sampson won the role of Jack Nicholson's mute Indian friend—and was an instant success when the film was released.

Jack Nicholson (left) and Will Sampson (right) in a scene from their movie One Flew Over the Cuckoo's Nest

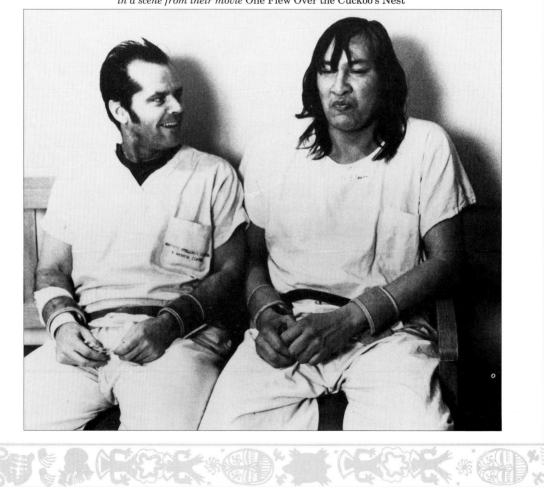

Other movie roles followed in quick succession. Besides *One Flew Over the Cuckoo's Nest*, Sampson's film credits include *The Outlaw Josey Wales* (1976), *Buffalo Bill and the Indians* (1976), *The White Buffalo* (1977), *Orca* (1977), *Alcatraz: The Whole Shocking Story* (1978), *Insignificance* (1986), and *Poltergeist II: The Other Side* (1986).

In all his roles, Sampson insisted on playing Indians as real, multidimensional characters. Scorning the traditional Hollywood stereotypes of Indians as either noble red men or savage red skins, Sampson played Indians as people, with a full range of complex emotions, motivations, and behaviors. Even though his methods were honored and his views sought (scriptwriters frequently consulted him about the accuracy of their Indian details), Sampson knew that Hollywood writers and directors had a long way to go before American Indians would be viewed as more than cartoon caricatures. As he once scornfully explained to a *New York Times* reporter, "They're still using 'em as livestock. They somehow just can't seem to bring it around to give the truth about Indians."

It was to hasten this truth that Sampson founded, in 1983, the American Indian Registry for the Performing Arts. Its objectives were simple—to establish and develop a central registry of American Indian performers and technical personnel in the entertainment field. The registry's other services include disseminating information, offering casting assistance, and encouraging cultural accuracy.

To further the American Indian cause, Sampson frequently spoke to schools and prisons about the plight of the contemporary Indian, and about the deepseated prejudice he felt still existed towards his people. Recognizing that many American Indians suffered from alcoholism, Sampson also channeled a portion of his movie earnings to a California enterprise called Red Wind, which offers assistance to Indians with substance-abuse problems.

Throughout his life, Sampson remained unimpressed with his own success as a movie actor. As he once explained to a reporter, "Movies offer me a lot of time to paint." He considered himself first and foremost a Muscogee and an artist, with acting coming in a distant third. As a painter, his one-man shows were well received, and his works have been exhibited at the Smithsonian, the Library of Congress, and museums across the country.

Still, to the general public, Will Sampson was known primarily as an unusually memorable screen actor. He brought new depths of realism and sensitivity to roles that had traditionally been seen as dull and unimaginative.

Will Sampson died on June 3, 1987, of complications after a heart-lung transplant. He is buried in Grave Creek Indian Cemetery in the heart of the Muscogee Nation.

Wilma Mankiller

Principal chief of Cherokee Nation
1945–

Wilma Mankiller has a job that she compares with being the president of a small country, the top executive of a corporation, and a social worker—all at the same time. She is the elected tribal leader of the Cherokee Nation of Oklahoma, the second-largest Indian nation in the United States, and she is the first woman ever to win that position. Chief Mankiller, with her soft voice and quiet manner, is steadily and successfully meeting the challenge of improving the lives of the Cherokee people, especially by developing their economic self-sufficiency and educational opportunities.

Wilma Pearl Mankiller (her last name is from an eighteenth-century warrior ancestor) has a long history of successfully meeting challenges. She grew up in rural poverty. Her early life did not seem to guide her toward political leadership. She was one of eleven children born to a poor farming family in Tahlequah, Oklahoma. Her mother was Dutch-Irish and her father, Cherokee. He was the descendant of people who were forced by the U.S. government to leave their homes in the southern Appalachians in 1838–1839 and make a life-threatening journey to Oklahoma. Family stories still recall the migration of her ancestors that is known as the Trail of Tears.

Despite living without electricity and running water, Wilma and her family were happy. Then when she was twelve, they moved to San Francisco. They moved as part of a Bureau of Indian Affairs program to relocate, or "mainstream," reservation Indians into cities. Mainstreaming was supposed to improve Indian people's lives, but the changes proved very stressful. The Mankiller family had to adjust to many new things while living in a housing project in a dangerous neighborhood of San Francisco. They missed the land and the people they had known in Oklahoma. But thanks especially to Wilma's father, they still managed to maintain their sense of Cherokee identity.

Wilma finished high school and went on to study sociology at San Francisco State University. Then she married an Ecuadoran businessman and had two daughters. In 1969, she became interested in politics when a group of Indian activists took over the abandoned prison island of Alcatraz, in San Francisco Bay. They were protesting U.S. government treatment of Indians. Their actions set her to thinking in new ways and helped her decide to change the direction of her own life. Remembering both the Trail of Tears and her own difficult experiences caused by the government policy of relocation, she, too, became an activist.

In 1976, with her marriage ended, Wilma Mankiller moved back to Tahlequah with her children. She began to devote her energies to the Cherokee nation, while continuing with her studies. She worked in community development, a field where she had ample opportunity to communicate a principle she believed in: self-help builds self-esteem.

Wilma Mankiller became involved in grass-roots activities to improve people's basic living conditions. She helped people initiate and carry out their own projects to repair old houses and build new ones. She worked to develop water systems in rural areas, so people could have running water in their homes. And she became very good at writing applications for federal grants to provide money for community projects like these. One of her successful applications brought funding to start Cherokee Gardens, which became a thriving commercial tree nursery employing many Cherokees.

One person who appreciated her abilities was Ross Swimmer, then the principal chief of the Cherokees. In 1983, when he was running for reelection, he asked her to run as deputy chief. They won the election. In 1985, Swimmer accepted the job of Commissioner of the Bureau of Indian Affairs, in Washington, D.C., and Wilma Mankiller took over as principal chief.

Wilma P. Mankiller is the first woman chief of the Cherokee Nation.

At first, some people were uncomfortable with a woman as chief. They were forgetting that historically the role of women in Cherokee affairs was very important. Traditionally, the Cherokees trace their family ancestry through the mother's clan, not the father's. Before the Cherokees left their homeland in the southeastern United States, women held power and made many decisions related to governing the tribe. Only after the Cherokees had contact with white settlers did Cherokees adopt a male-centered political system. So Wilma Mankiller's leadership role was both a step into the future and a reuniting with the past for her people.

By 1987, when she ran for reelection as principal chief, the doubters had been quieted. In 1991, she was again reelected, this time by a landslide. Clearly the Cherokees felt she was serving them well and should continue to lead their fight against poverty and discouragement.

Some of the greatest challenges Wilma Mankiller has faced during her career have had to do with injury and illness. In 1979, she was in a terrible car accident. Recovery took many months, and she had to have seventeen operations to repair problems. During this time she discovered she had myasthenia gravis, a serious disease of the nervous system. Treatment meant more surgery and a long program of chemotherapy. More recently she has undergone a kidney transplant, receiving a kidney given by her brother.

Wilma Mankiller feels she has overcome these challenges with the help of the same traditional Cherokee wisdom that can heal the whole Cherokee community. Have a good mind, the Cherokee elders say: find what is good in a situation or person, and respond to the good part. Remember that we all depend on each other. And always look out for the future: think of how choices made now will affect even those who will be living seven generations from now. To these Wilma Mankiller might have added the comment she made to a *Newsweek* reporter asking about Cherokee successes in economic development: "Our secret is that we never, never give up."

AIM

The American Indian Movement (AIM) is both an organization and the philosophy the organization represents. In simple terms, AIM reminds the U.S. government to uphold treaties and other obligations to Indian people. Especially during the 1970s, AIM played an important role in bringing the neglected issues of Indian rights to the public's attention. Some of AIM's methods and actions, however, have provoked criticism, from inside as well as outside the Indian community.

AIM developed from the Red Power movement that surfaced after World War II. Red Power sought to resist white domination of Indian culture by getting different Indian groups to cooperate in improving their own economic and educational status. Several organizations across the political spectrum grew up around this basic idea.

Lakota stand guard over the Sacred Heart Catholic Church in Wounded Knee.

Some of the AIM members used crossbows with arrows to hold Wounded Knee in 1973.

The AIM organization was probably the most forceful group to emerge from the Red Power movement. It was founded in Minneapolis in 1968 by young urban Indian activists. AIM began as an organization to watch police patrols in Indian neighborhoods where there were many reports of police harrassment. With AIM monitoring police activities, reports of discriminatory arrests dropped sharply. After this success, AIM activists became concerned with other kinds of urban problems such as unemployment and housing. They conducted protests and sometimes got arrested, but they also got plenty of publicity for their viewpoint.

More press coverage led to more followers, new chapters were opened in other cities and states, and AIM activities broadened. Founders Dennis Banks and Charles Mitchell, together with Clyde and Virgil Bellecourt, all Ojibwas, and Russell Means, an Oglala Sioux, became recognized as the AIM leadership and spokesmen. From 1969 to 1971, AIM took part in the occupation of Alcatraz, the former prison island in San Francisco Bay. Protesters intended that their civil disobedience would call attention to Indian struggles for freedom. They eventually gave up the occupation, but not before they had stirred the imaginations of many people around the county who felt a kinship with the cause.

Other occupations and takeovers followed. A keynote of these was nationalism—a demand that Indian tribes be recognized as independent, sovereign nations as stated in existing treaties with the U.S. government. In 1971, AIM organized an occupation of Mt. Rushmore, the huge granite memorial to Washington, Jefferson, Lincoln, and Theodore Roosevelt carved into the Black Hills of South Dakota. AIM demanded that the U.S. government restore terms of the 1868 Treaty of Fort Laramie and return the Black Hills to the Lakota.

In 1972, taking advantage of the publicity potential in the upcoming presidential election, AIM held a cross-country march on Washington called the Trail of Broken Treaties. Activists met at the Bureau of Indian Affairs (BIA) with a list of demands that centered around Indian sovereignty. When government officials refused to go along, the protesters seized control of the building and BIA offices were vandalized.

Many people became uncomfortable with AIM because of these and other protests. They were put off by all the tough talk, the use of violence, the threatening way members sometimes waved about their weapons. Other more conservative observers on reservations could not agree with AIM's analysis of the situation facing Indians or with AIM's proposed solutions. Support for and interest in AIM faltered. Another setback came with AIM's best-publicized action—the occupation of the town of Wounded Knee in 1973. Trouble related to the Wounded Knee protest continued for years.

Yet AIM's actions during this era prompted beneficial changes in BIA officers, policies, tribal leadership, and funding levels. Media attention to AIM stimulated ethnic pride and helped make America much more aware of Indian issues.

Although it is not featured in the national news as often, and its membership has declined in recent years, AIM is still pursuing the goals of promoting Indian self-determination and gaining recognition for treaty rights. AIM includes among its activities a variety of community programs that deserve more publicity than they receive. These programs bring charitable, educational, and children's services to Indians where they live. Today's AIM is as likely to offer nutrition and childcare advice as it is to promote a political viewpoint. AIM also provides speakers for community functions, and it keeps historical records and compiles statistical information about Indians. Most recently, AIM has been emphasizing ecology, ritual, and cosmic harmony.

Indians stand vigil in their takeover of Wounded Knee.

Donald Pelotte
Abenaki Roman Catholic bishop
1945–

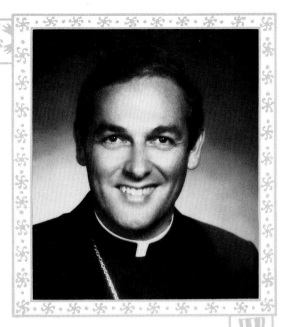

The Most Reverend Donald E. Pelotte had just stepped out of a swimming pool when the telephone rang. The caller was Archbishop Pio Laghi, official ambassador of Pope John Paul II in the United States. The Archbishop's message was simple and awesome. Reverend Pelotte had just been appointed Coadjutor Bishop of the Gallup diocese of New Mexico and Arizona. With this phone call, Donald Pelotte became the first American Indian Catholic bishop in U.S. history.

Bishop Pelotte traveled a long road to reach this junction. He was born on April 13, 1945, the youngest (with his twin brother Dana) of five sons born to Norris and Margaret Pelotte. Donald's father was Abenaki of the Algonquin nation in the northeastern United States and Canada; his mother was of French-Canadian descent.

Donald's parents were divorced when he and Dana were only a few months old, and the children were raised by their mother in and around Waterville, Maine. It was a hard life. Money was scarce, and the family depended on generous neighbors and welfare benefits to make ends meet. Frequently, all five boys shared the same bed in an effort to stay warm during the harsh Maine winters.

Donald's mother was a devout Catholic, and she raised her boys to be the same. From the time Donald used to wake at dawn to serve as an altar boy, he knew he wanted to be a priest. After graduating from high school at Eymard Seminary in Hyde Park, New York, he attended John Carroll University in

Cleveland, Ohio, and earned a B.A. degree in philosophy in 1969. While studying for the priesthood at Blessed Sacrament Seminary, he completed his doctoral studies at Fordham University in New York; he was ordained a priest in 1972 and earned a Ph.D. in Theology in 1975.

In 1978, Pelotte was named provincial superior of the Blessed Sacrament congregation in suburban Cleveland, Ohio. At thirty-three, he was the youngest provincial superior in the country. His work took him to such places as east Africa, Vietnam, the Philippines, England, and Ireland.

*Bishop Pelotte during the
ceremony that elevated him to the position of Bishop*

But nothing he had done in the comfortable suburbs of Cleveland quite prepared Bishop Pelotte for the task confronting him in Gallup. The Gallup diocese is physically the largest in America, covering some 55,000 square miles of desert and mountain territory in New Mexico and Arizona. It is also the diocese with the largest concentration of Catholic Indians. Bishop Pelotte knew he had much to learn about the customs and lifestyles of the large American Indian and Hispanic population in his new congregation.

Bishop Pelotte lost no time familiarizing himself with the traditions and values of his congregants. His ordination Mass as a bishop in May 1986 combined standard Catholic liturgy with the chants and dances of the Navajo, Pueblo, and Apache tribes native to the region.

Pelotte recognizes that his task will not be easy. "One of the problems with Catholicism," he says, "is that so often we equate it with Western culture." For five hundred years, Catholic missionaries of all nationalities have tried to change the traditional beliefs of American Indians. It is only recently that the Church has recognized the importance of respecting and integrating American Indian spirituality with Catholic spirituality.

It is in acknowledgment of this need that Bishop Pelotte has, since 1981, been a national board member of the Tekakwitha Conference, an organization for American Indian Catholics. A recent concern of this organization was the commemoration of the 500th anniversary of Columbus's arrival in what Europeans called the New World—and what American Indians called home. After working for three years with U.S. bishops on a pastoral letter commemorating the fifth centenary of Christianity in America, Pelotte's persistent influence paid off. The original title of the letter, "Sounding the Jubilee Horn," was changed to "Heritage and Hope: Evangelism in the United States." The body of the letter, too, was changed to include an apology to Indians for the church's disregard of traditional Indian spirituality.

Despite the difficulty in reconciling his beliefs as a Catholic priest with his American Indian heritage, Bishop Pelotte is confident that such a reconciliation is possible. As he once wrote, "As a Native American, I have been privileged to share in the annual gatherings of the Jesuits in Native North American Ministries . . . I have found there a sense of real companionship rooted in common concerns and a common reverence for the Native peoples and cultures. I truly believe that our often unheard voices have much to say to the larger U.S. society about care for the environment, about what it truly means to live in community, about spirituality, and about coming to know the true self in the presence of the divine."

Bishop Donald E. Pelotte calls for a new era in Indian/Catholic understanding, greater commitment to American Indians' struggle for justice, and greater respect for and sensitivity to their traditional ways of life. He offers hope to people as he daily lives up to his episcopal motto, "Strengthen One Another."

æ æ æ æ

Joy Harjo
Muscogee (Creek) poet and screenwriter
1951–

When you read Joy Harjo's poems, you may feel stirred or disturbed. Her writing often has layers of meaning, and she tells you about hard-to-get-hold-of things: the spirit selves of people, the importance of memory and speaking, the experience of being an Indian, the experience of being a woman. Sometimes her words show you fear and hatred, but she also shows you transforming visions of harmony and liberation.

Joy Harjo is one of America's most talented young poets. Her early years were troubled and impoverished, but as a poet she has turned those experiences into something powerful and useful. To date, she has produced four books of poetry and one of prose.

Originally from Tulsa, Oklahoma, Joy Harjo is the eldest of four children of a Muscogee (Creek) father and a French-Cherokee mother. Joy lived in Tulsa until she was sixteen. Today, she still feels very connected to the people, stories, and places of her childhood, and to the Muscogee part of her heritage. Her Muscogee ancestors lived in Alabama, and her great-great-grandfather led a war resisting the U.S. government's attempts to remove the Muscogee from their traditional lands. In 1832, he and his family were forced to move to Indian Territory. Memories of that terrible time echo in her poetry.

Ever since childhood, Joy Harjo has liked drawing. When she was little, she wanted to be an artist. Her grandmother, Namomi Harjo, and her aunt, Lois Harjo, were both artists and provided the examples she needed to encourage her talent. Joy attended high school in Santa Fe, New Mexico, at the Institute of American Indian Arts. Later she studied fine arts at the University of New Mexico in Albuquerque. It was at the university where Joy says "poetry-speaking 'called me' . . . and I couldn't say no." Words, she began to feel, would let her say more than painting, so Joy switched into a creative-writing program, and went on to get a graduate degree in creative writing at the University of Iowa. Since then, she has taught literature and creative writing at several universities in the West. Presently she is back in Albuquerque, where she is a professor at the University of New Mexico.

Filmmaking is another intense interest for Joy Harjo. Her imagination is very visual, as her early attraction to drawing demonstrated. Screenwriting, she feels, is closely related to writing poetry, because both involve translating emotions into images, one in terms of pictures, the other in terms of language. She is a consultant for the Native American Public Broadcasting Consortium, and has written several scripts for films released by that organization.

In addition, Joy Harjo is active in community service. She has served on boards and panels for such organizations as the National Association for Third World Writers, the National Endowment for the Arts, and the En'owkin Centre International School of Writing. She has also worked with and contributed to several literary journals.

All these activities make clear that Joy Harjo has a busy career. Yet she has managed many of her accomplishments while also being the single mother of two children. She says she has tried to live a life that would be a positive influence for them. She is also a musician and plays saxophone with her band, Poetic Justice.

Here is "Remember," which Harjo has revised from her 1983 book *She Had Some Horses*. In this poem are some of the themes that appear in her work: the significance of memory, kinship, and language, and the linkage between the natural world and human lives. She tells us to cherish and pay attention to these things, because they are what make us who we are.

Remember the sky that you were born under,
know each of the star's stories.

Remember the moon, know who she is.

Remember the sun's birth at dawn, that is the
strongest point of time.

Remember sundown
and the giving away to night.

Remember your birth, how your mother struggled
to give you form and breath. You are evidence of
her life, and her mother's, and hers.

Remember your father. He is your life, also.

Remember the earth whose skin you are:
red earth, black earth, yellow earth, white earth
brown earth, we are earth.

Remember the plants, trees, animal life who all have their
tribes, their families, their histories, too. Talk to them,
listen to them. They are alive poems.

Remember the wind.

Remember her voice. She knows
the origin of this universe.

Remember, you are all people and that all people
are you.

Remember, you are this universe and that this
universe is you.

Remember, all is in motion, is growing, is you.

Remember, language comes from this.

Remember the dance that language is, that life is.

Remember.

&a &a &a &a

Louise Erdrich

Ojibwa (Chippewa) fiction writer and poet
1954–

Michael Dorris

Modoc anthropologist and writer
1945–

They make a remarkable team. They work together, both in the difficult processes of writing books and in a real-life marriage. Louise Erdrich and Michael Dorris are probably better known to the reading public than any other contemporary writers with American Indian roots. Some of their ideas derive from their Indian heritage, but the vividly imagined characters they create have universal appeal.

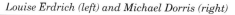

Louise Erdrich (left) and Michael Dorris (right)

Dorris and Erdrich first met each other when she was an undergraduate student at Dartmouth College, in New Hampshire, and he was a young faculty member there. Romance and writing together did not develop until several years later.

Erdrich came to Dartmouth from North Dakota. She had grown up in the small town of Wahpeton, near a reservation where her parents taught at a Bureau of Indian Affairs boarding school. Her mother was Ojibwa—her mother's father was tribal chairman of the Turtle Mountain Reservation in North Dakota—and her father was of German descent. Erdrich was the oldest of seven children in a "chaotic, pretty typical" household. Although Erdrich attended the Indian boarding school, she says she never thought much about her family's background when she was young. But at an early age she came to think of herself as a writer, something her parents encouraged. When she was a child, her father would pay her a nickel for every story she wrote, and her mother would help her make construction-paper covers for her "books." It was at Dartmouth that Erdrich first became interested in her native heritage. She majored in English and creative writing, but also took a course taught by Michael Dorris.

Dorris was a professor of anthropology and Native American studies. Born in Louisville, Kentucky, he also lived in Idaho, Washington, and Montana while he was growing up. His father was a Modoc, a member of a small Indian nation originally native to northern California and southern Oregon. He studied English and related subjects in college and in graduate school at Yale University. Dorris had written some poems and short stories but didn't think of himself as a writer. Instead, he was focused on anthropology and the study of American Indians.

In 1972, Dartmouth hired Dorris to develop a new program of courses in the field of Native American studies. During the mid-1970s, Dorris, still a bachelor, adopted three Indian children. Between raising the children and his academic career, he was deeply involved in a busy, fulfilling life.

In 1979, Erdrich and Dorris renewed their acquaintance when Erdrich returned to Dartmouth on a brief visit. After graduating from Dartmouth, Louise held a variety of jobs, earned a master's degree in creative writing, and began to develop a reputation as a fine poet. She and Michael Dorris began to exchange letters and long comments on drafts of each others' writing. Through the mail, the relationship deepened, and they realized they wanted to get married. Since their marriage in 1981, they have become the parents of three more children. In addition, five novels, a book of nonfiction, two books of poetry, and a good number of short stories and magazine articles have been published with one or both of their names listed as authors.

Dorris and Erdrich published their first novel together, The Crown of Columbus, *in 1991.*

Their home is in Kalispel, Montana. Aside from the occasional clattering of the youngest children, it is mostly a quiet life. They write separately, but trade their work back and forth, penciling in comments and rewriting, sometimes many times. And they talk a lot—about everything from exact wording, to how best to organize a paragraph or chapter, to imagined details like what a story's characters wear, or their favorite colors, or what they might order in a restaurant. By the time a piece of writing leaves their house, Erdrich and Dorris have both influenced everything about it, regardless of whose name appears as author.

This process has worked well. During the 1980s, Erdrich completed three novels of a planned series of four inspired by her North Dakota background. Some of the characters, who include Indians and non-Indians, turn up in more than one book. Together, the novels describe the complex relationships over time among a group of often eccentric individuals and families. Dorris's novel is also about a memorable Indian family, and deals with women of three generations. His 1989 nonfiction work, the award-winning book *The Broken Cord*, centers on one of the children he adopted and the effects suffered by the boy because of his birth mother's drinking. Dorris and Erdrich's most recent book, and the first to carry both their names, is *The Crown of Columbus*, a four-hundred page novel whose main characters are contemporary American Indians.

The books that Louise Erdrich and Michael Dorris have produced have been popular with readers and acclaimed by literary critics. Erdrich has said that she and Dorris have ideas for more projects than they could ever complete. Although Erdrich and Dorris devote much of their time to writing, they are both active lecturers and work to support critical issues such as land restoration and fetal alcohol syndrome/effect prevention.

❧ ❧ ❧ ❧

For Further Reading

(U) = Upper Grades   (M) = Middle Grades

Biography

Anderson, Peter. Charles Eastman: *Physician, Reformer, and Native American Leader.* Chicago: Childrens Press, 1992. (M)

Black, Sheila. *Sitting Bull: And the Battle of Little Big Horn.* Englewood Cliffs, NJ: Silver Burdett Press, 1989. (M)

Brown, Marian Marsh. *Sacagawea: Indian Interpreter to Lewis and Clark.* Chicago: Childrens Press, 1988. (M)

Brown, Marian Marsh. *Susette La Flesche: Advocate for Native American Rights.* Chicago: Childrens Press, 1992. (M)

Eastman, Charles A. *From the Deep Woods to Civilization: Chapters in the Autobiography of an Indian.* Lincoln: University of Nebraska Press, 1977. (U)

Fox, Mary Virginia. *Chief Joseph of the Nez Perce Indians: Champion of Liberty.* Chicago: Childrens Press, 1992. (M)

Fritz, Jean. *The Double Life of Pocahontas.* New York: The Putnam Publishing Group, 1983. (M)

Gonzales, Catherine Troy. *Quanah Parker: Great Chief of the Comanches.* Austin, TX: Eakin Press, 1987. (M)

Katz, Jane B., ed. *This Song Remembers: Self-Portraits of Native Americans in the Arts.* Boston: Houghton Mifflin, 1980. (M)

Keith, Harold. *Will Rogers, A Boy's Life: An Indian Territory Childhood.* Reprint of the 1937 edition. Norman, OK: Levite Apache Publishing, 1991. (M)

Marriott, Alice. *Maria: The Potter of San Ildefonso.* (Civilization of the American Indian Series: Vol. 27) Norman: University of Oklahoma Press, 1987. (U)

Milstein, David R. *Will Rogers: An Appreciation.* Bowling Green Station, NY: Gordon Press, 1976. (U)

Richards, Gregory. *Jim Thorpe: World's Greatest Athlete.* Chicago: Childrens Press, 1986. (M)

Rogers, Betty. *Will Rogers*. Norman: University of Oklahoma Press, 1982. (U)

Rollins, Peter C. *Will Rogers: A Bio-Bibliography*. Westport, CT: Greenwood Press, 1984. (U)

History

Ashabranner, Brent. *Morning Star, Black Sun: The Northern Cheyenne Indians and America's Energy Crisis*. New York: Putnam Publishing Group, 1982. (U)

Ashabranner, Brent. *To Live in Two Worlds: American Indian Youth Today*. New York: Dodd, Mead, 1984. (M)

Behrens, June. *Powwow*. Chicago: Childrens Press, 1983. (M)

Beyer, Don E. *The Totem Pole Indians of the Northwest*. New York: Franklin Watts. (M)

Brown, Dee. *Wounded Knee: An Indian History of the American West*. New York: Dell, 1975. (U)

Brown, Virginia and Laurella Owens. *The World of the Southern Indians*. Birmingham, AL: Beechwood Books, 1983. (M)

Burrill, Richard L. *Ishi: America's Last Stone Age Indian*. Sacramento: Antro Co., 1990. (M)

Carter, Alden R. *The Shoshoni*. New York: Franklin Watts, 1991. (M)

Cohen, Fay G. and Jeanne Heuving, eds. *Tribal Sovereignty: Indian Tribes in U.S. History*. Seattle, WA: Daybreak Star Press, 1981. (M)

Cwiklik, Robert. *Sequoia*. Englewood Cliffs, NJ: Silver Burdett Press, 1989. (M)

Deloria, Vine, Jr., ed. *American Indian Policy in the Twentieth Century*. Norman: University of Oklahoma Press, 1985. (U)

Deloria, Vine, Jr. *Behind the Trail of Broken Treaties: An Indian Declaration of Independence*. Norman: University of Texas Press, 1985. (U)

Deloria, Vine, Jr. *Custer Died for Your Sins: An Indian Manifesto*. Norman: University of Oklahoma Press, 1988. (U)

Dockstader, Frederick J. *The Kachina & The White Man: The Influence of White Culture on the Hopi Kachina Culture*. Albuquerque: University of New Mexico Press, 1985. (U)

Doherty, Craig A. & Katherine M. *The Apaches and Navajos*. New York: Franklin Watts, 1989. (M)

Doherty, Craig A. & Katherine M. *The Iroquois*. New York: Franklin Watts, 1989. (M)

Dorris, Michael. *The Broken Cord: A Family's Ongoing Struggle with Fetal Alcohol Syndrome*. New York: HarperCollins, 1989. (U)

Freedman, Russell. *Buffalo Hunt*. New York: Holiday House, 1988. (M)

Freedman, Russell. *Indian Chiefs*. New York: Holiday House, 1987. (U)

Greene, Jacqueline D. *The Maya*. New York: Franklin Watts, 1992. (M)

Highwater, Jamake. *Many Smokes, Many Moons: A Chronology of American Indian History Through Art*. New York: HarperCollins, 1978. (U)

Hirschfelder, Arlene. *Happily May I Walk: American Indians and Alaska Natives Today*. New York: Scribner, 1986. (U)

Katz, William Loren. *Black Indians: A Hidden Heritage*. New York: Athenaeum, 1986. (U)

La Flesche, Francis. *A Dictionary of the Osage Language*. Brighton, MI: Native American Book Publishers, 1990. (U)

Landau, Elaine. *The Cherokees*. New York: Franklin Watts, 1992. (M)

Landau, Elaine. *The Sioux*. New York: Franklin Watts, 1991. (M)

Lee, Martin. *The Seminoles*. New York: Franklin Watts, 1989. (M)

Liptak, Karen. *North American Indian Ceremonies*. New York: Franklin Watts, 1992. (M)

Liptak, Karen. *North American Indian Medicine People*. New York: Franklin Watts, 1990. (M)

Liptak, Karen. *North American Indian Sign Language*. New York: Franklin Watts, 1990. (M)

Liptak, Karen. *North American Indian Survival Skills*. New York: Franklin Watts, 1990. (M)

Liptak, Karen. *North American Indian Tribal Chiefs*. New York: Franklin Watts, 1992. (M)

McLain, Gary. *The Indian Way: Learning to Communicate with Mother Earth*. Santa Fe, NM: John Muir Publications, 1990. (U)

Myers, Arthur. *The Cheyenne*. New York: Franklin Watts, 1992. (M)

New Mexico People and Energy Collective. *Red Ribbon for Emma*. Berkeley, CA: New Seed Press, 1981. (M)

Newman, Shirlee P. *The Incas*. New York: Franklin Watts, 1992. (M)

Ortiz, Simon. *The People Shall Continue*. Revised Edition. San Francisco: Children's Book Press, 1988. (U)

Quiri, Patricia Ryon. *The Algonquians*. New York: Franklin Watts, 1992. (M)

Shepherd, Donna Walsh. *The Aztecs*. New York: Franklin Watts, 1992. (M)

United Indians of All Tribes Foundation. *Sharing Our Worlds: Native American Children Today*. Seattle, WA: Daybreak Star Press, 1980. (M)

Wolfson, Evelyn. *American Indian Tools and Ornaments: How to Make Implements and Jewelry with Bone and Shell*. New York: Random House/David McKay, 1981. (M)

Wolfson, Evelyn. *From Abenaki to Zuni: A Dictionary of Native American Tribes*. New York: Walker & Co., 1988. (M)

Wunder, John R. *The Kiowa*. New York: Chelsea House, 1989. (U)

Fiction, Poetry

Allen, Terry, ed. *The Whispering Wind: Poetry by Young American Indians*. New York: Doubleday, 1972. (U)

Baylor, Byrd. *A God on Every Mountain Top*. New York, Charles Scribner's Sons, 1981. (M)

Cannon, A.E. *The Shadow Brothers*. New York: Doubleday, 1990. (U)

DeFelice, Cynthia. *Weasel*. New York: MacMillan, 1990. (M)

Dorris, Michael. *A Yellow Raft in Blue Water*. New York: Warner Books, 1988. (U)

Erdrich, Louise. *The Beet Queen*. New York: Henry Holt & Company, 1986. (U)

Erdrich, Louise. *Love Medicine*. New York: Henry Holt & Company, 1984. (U)

Erdrich, Louise. *Tracks*. New York: Henry Holt & Company, 1988. (U)

George, Jean Craighead. *Julie of the Wolves*. New York: HarperCollins, 1972. (U)

George, Jean Craighead. *The Talking Earth*. New York: HarperCollins, 1987. (M)

Gregory, Kristiana. *Jenny of the Tetons*. San Diego: Harcourt Brace Jovanovich, 1989. (U)

Harjo, Joy. *In Mad Love & War*. Hanover, NH: University Press of New England, 1990. (U)

Harjo, Joy. *She Had Some Horses*. New York: Thunder's Mouth Press, 1983. (U)

Highwater, Jamke. *ANPAO: An American Indian Odyssey*. New York: Harper Collins, 1977. (U)

Highwater, Jamke. *The Ceremony of Innocence*. New York: HarperCollins, 1985. (U)

Highwater, Jamke. *Legend Days*. New York: HarperCollins, 1984. (U)

Hobbs, Will. *Bearstone*. New York: Avon Books, 1991. (U)

Momaday, N. Scott. *The Ancient Child*. New York: Doubleday, 1989. (U)

Momaday, N. Scott. *The Way To Rainy Mountain*. Albuquerque: University of New Mexico Press, 1976. (U)

O'Dell, Scott. *Black Star, Bright Dawn*. Boston: Houghton Mifflin, 1988. (U)

Pitts, Paul. *Racing the Sun*. New York: Avon Books, 1988. (M)

Sneve, Virginia Driving Hawk, ed. *Dancing Teepees: Poems of American Indian Youth*. New York: Holiday House, 1989. (U)

Speare, Elizabeth George. *The Sign of the Beaver*. Boston: Houghton Mifflin, 1983. (M)

Wallin, Luke. *Ceremony of the Panther*. New York: Bradbury Press, 1987. (U)

Wisler, G. Clifton. *The Raid*. New York: Dutton/Lodestar, 1985. (U)

Worcester, Donald. *Lone Hunter's Gray Pony*. Fort Worth: Texas Christian University Press, 1985. (M)

Wosmek, Frances. *A Brown Bird Singing*. New York: Lothrop, Lee & Shepard, 1986. (M)

Folktales, Myths

Bierhorst, John, ed. *The Mythology of North America*. New York: William Morrow, 1985. (U)

Bierhorst, John, ed. *The Sacred Path: Spells, Prayers, and Power Songs of the American Indians*. New York: William Morrow, 1983. (M)

Bruchac, Joseph. *The Faithful Hunter: Abenaki Stories*. Greenfield Review Literary Center, 1989. (U)

Bruchac, Joseph. *Iroquois Stories: Heroes & Heroines, Monsters & Magic*. Bowen, CO: Crossing Press, 1985. (U)

Bruchac, Joseph. *Native American Stories*. Golden, CO: Fulcrum Publishing, 1991. (U)

Bruchac, Joseph. *Return of the Sun: Native American Tales from the Northeast Woodlands.* Crossing Press, 1989. (U)

Eastman, Charles A. *Wigwam Evenings: Sioux Tales Retold.* Lincoln: University of Nebraska Press, 1977. (U)

Gifford, Barry, ed. *Selected Writings of Edward S. Curtis.* Berkeley, CA: Creative Arts, 1976. (U)

Goble, Paul. *Star Boy.* New York: Bradbury Press, 1983. (M)

Halverson, Lydia, illustrator. *The Animals' Ballgame.* (Picturebook with audiocassette.) Chicago: Childrens Press, 1992. (M)

Mayo, Gretchen Will. *Earthmaker's Tales: North American Indian Stories about Earth Happenings.* New York: Walker & Company, 1987. (M)

Monroe, Jean Guard and Ray A. Williamson. *They Dance in the Sky: Native American Star Myths.* Boston: Houghton Mifflin, 1987. (U)

Nelson, Anita, illustrator. *Loon and Deer Were Traveling.* (Picturebook with audiocassette.) Chicago: Childrens Press, 1992. (M)

Regan, Rick, illustrator. *The Naughty Little Rabbit and Old Man Coyote.* (Picturebook with audiocassette.) Chicago: Childrens Press, 1992. (M)

Skivington, Janice, illustrator. *The Girl from the Sky.* (Picturebook with audiocassette.) Chicago: Childrens Press, 1992. (M)

Shetterly, S.H. *Raven's Light: A Myth from the People of the Northwest Coast.* New York: Athenaeum, 1991. (M)

Te Ata. *Baby Rattlesnake.* Adapted by Lynn Moroney. San Francisco: Children's Book Press, 1989. (M)

Videotapes

Ancient Spirit, Living Word: The Oral Tradition. Produced by KBDI-TV, 1983.

Folklore of the Muscogee (Creek) People. Produced by Gary Robinson, Creek Nation Communications and KOED-TV, Tulsa, Oklahoma, 1983.

Gifts of Santa Fe. Produced by Marguerite J. Moritz, 1988. Tells the story of the Santa Fe Indian Market, an annual gathering of the most prestigious Native American artists in the world.

Herman Red Elk: A Sioux Indian Artist. Produced by South Dakota ETV, 1975.

I Am Different from My Brother: Dakota Name-Giving. Produced by NAPBC, 1981.

Indian Arts at the Phoenix Herd Museum. Produced by KAET-TV, 1975. A six-part series exploring the six major areas of Native American art: basketry, painting, pottery, textiles, jewelry, kachinas.

Mother Corn. Produced by KBYU-TV, 1977. Explores the historical significances of various types of corn among Native American cultures.

Nations Within a Nation. Produced by the Department of Sociology, Oklahoma State University, 1986. Examines the issue of sovereignty in Native American communities.

Native American Images. Produced by Carol Patton, Cornsilk/Southwest Texas Public Broadcasting Council, 1984. Profiles of artists Paladine H. Roye, Donald Vann, Steve Forbes.

Navajo. Produced by KBYU-TV, 1979.

Navajo Code Talkers. Produced by Tom McCarthy and KENW-TV, 1986.

1,000 Years of Muscogee (Creek) Art. Produced by Gary Robinson, Creek Nation Communications, 1982.

Oscar Howe: The Sioux Painter. Produced by KUSD-TV, 1973.

Seasons of a Navajo. Produced by Peace River Films and KAET-TV, 1984.

The Sun Dagger. Produced by The Solstice Project, 1983. Explores the Anasazi culture and their remarkable carved calendar marking solstices, equinoxes, and the nineteen-year lunar cycle.

The Treaty of 1868. Produced by NETCHE, 1987. A two-part series examining the debate over who really owns the Black Hills of western South Dakota.

The Trial of Standing Bear. Produced by Nebraska ETV, 1988.

White Man's Way. Produced by Christine Lesiak, Nebraska ETV, 1986. An examination of the Genoa, Nebraska U.S. Indian School, a government-supported military-style school where Indian children were taught the white man's language and lifestyle and forbidden to practice their own.

All videotapes are available from the Native American Public Broadcasting Consortium, Inc., P.O. Box 83111, Lincoln, Nebraska 68501-3111, 402-472-3522.

Index

Acknowledgments

Cover photographs, left to right, top to bottom: R.H. Lowie Museum, University of California, Berkeley (Ishi); Culver Pictures (Sequoyah); Americans for Indian Opportunity (LaDonna Harris); The Bettmann Archive (Sitting Bull); Historical Pictures/Stock Montage (Charles Curtis); Culver Pictures (Jim Thorpe, Will Rogers); Museum of New Mexico (Maria Martinez); AP/Wide World (Maria Tallchief); UPI/Bettmann (Clarence Tinker); Culver Pictures (Tecumseh).

Historical Pictures/Stock Montage: ii, v, vi, ix, x, xx; North Wind Picture Archives: 2; Courtesy of the Detroit Historical Department; photo by Nemo Warr: 5; Historical Pictures/Stock Montage: 7; Courtesy Hampton House Studios, Inc.: 9; Courtesy Tennessee Department of Tourism: 10; North Wind Picture Archives: 13, 16; Culver Pictures: 18; North Wind Picture Archives: 19; Albany Institute of History & Art: 20; The New York Historical Society, New York City: 23; Culver Pictures: 26; Historical Pictures/Stock Montage: 29; Culver Pictures: 30; Historical Pictures/Stock Montage: 32, 34; North Wind Picture Archives: 36; Historical Pictures/Stock Montage: 38; Mark Segal/Tony Stone Worldwide: 40; North Wind Picture Archives: 43; Woolaroc Museum, Bartlesville, OK: 45; Historical Pictures/Stock Montage: 47, National Museum of American Art/Art Resource, NY: 49; North Wind Picture Archives: 50; Historical Pictures/Stock Montage: 53, The Bettmann Archive: 55; Courtesy, Colorado Historical Society: 59; UPI/ Bettmann: 61; Culver Pictures: 63; The Bettmann Archive: 65, 67; UPI/ Bettmann: 69, 71; Oregon Historical Society: 73; Historical Pictures/Stock Montage: 74; UPI/Bettmann: 79, 81, 83; Historical Pictures/Stock Montage: 85, 87, 89; Omaha World-Herald: 91; Nebraska State Historical Society: 93, 94; YMCA of the USA Archives, University of Minnesota Libraries: 96, 98; Historical Pictures/Stock Montage: 100; Smithsonian Institution National Anthropological Archives: 102; R.H. Lowie Museum, University of California, Berkeley: 104, 106; Smithsonian Institution: 108; Western Historical Manuscript Collection, University of Missouri, Columbia: 110; State Historical Society of South Dakota: 112; The Bettmann Archive: 114; UPI/ Bettmann: 117; Culver Pictures: 119, 120; Museum of New Mexico: 123; Arthur

Taylor/Museum of New Mexico: 124L, 124R; UPI/Bettmann: 126; Culver Pictures: 128, 130, 131; UPI/Bettmann: 133; The University of South Dakota: 136; Kenji Kerins: 139; Courtesy of Mel Lone Hill: 140, 142; Doug Thurston: 143; AP/Wide World: 146, 147, 148; Kim Jew: 150; National Museum of the American Indian, Smithsonian Institution: 151; The Philbrook Museum of Art, Tulsa: 152; University Art Galleries, University of South Dakota: 154; Collection of Inge Dawn Howe Maresh, 1992 Adelheid Howe: 156; Emmett P. Hadden/Museum of New Mexico: 160; Courtesy of Fred Dockstader: 162; John Running: 163; Courtesy Roderick RedElk: 166; AP/Wide World: 168, 170; The Gilcrease Museum, Tulsa: 171; Native American Rights Fund: 173; State of Idaho: 174; AP/Wide World: 176; Culver Pictures: 178; State Arts Council of Oklahoma: 179; UPI/Bettmann: 180; Kenji Kerins: 182; Americans for Indian Opportunity: 183, 184; University of Arizona: 186; North Wind Picture Archives: 188; UPI/Bettmann: 190, 191; Courtesy George Abrams: 193; Rafael Macia/Photo Researchers: 194; Marlene Foster: 196; Stephen Trimble: 198; AP/Wide World: 201; Courtesy of Ensign: 205; UPI/Bettmann: 206; Muscogee (Creek) Nation: 209; Memory Shop: 210; Cherokee Nation Communications: 213; Mark Myers/Photri, Inc.: 215; UPI/Bettmann: 217; AP/Wide World: 218, 220; The Gallup Diocese of New Mexico & Arizona: 221; John Zierten: 222; Robyn Stoutenburg: 225; James Woodcock: 229; Kenji Kerins: 231; Historical Pictures/Stock Montage: 252.

Consultants' Biographies

Dr. Jay Miller is a fellow at the D'Arcy McNickle Center for the History of the American Indian, Newberry Library, in Chicago. He received his doctorate from Rutgers University and wrote his dissertation on the Keres Pueblo (*The Anthropology of Keres Identity: A Structural Study of the Ethnographic and Archaeological Record of the Keres Pueblos*). Dr. Miller's other publications include *Shamanic Odyssey: The Lushootseed Salish Journey to the Land of the Dead, Mourning Dove: A Salishan Autobiography,* and *Tsimshian and Their Neighbors of the North Pacific Coast.*

Patricia Locke is a well-known journalist, humanitarian, orator, and activist. She was born on the Ft. Hall Reservation in Idaho in 1928; her father was White Earth Chippewa (Mississippi Band), and her mother was both Lakota and Dakota. As a child she lived in Arizona and Idaho and was exposed to the cultures of many Indian tribes. She also learned how to succeed in a non-Indian society. As a child she was ordered to sit in the "colored section" of a movie theater, and Pat's mother went to the theater owner and said, "If you continue to do this, I will tell all the Indians and my white friends not to go to your movies." Pat remembers her mother as "a brave-hearted woman." Pat Locke has made it her purpose to improve the quality of life for indigenous peoples by working with tribal governments as well as federal, state, and local governments to improve programs in education, native languages, mental health, drug and alcoholism prevention programs, and care for the elderly. Her numerous articles and papers have been published widely, and she has received many distinguished awards and appointments. In 1991 she was named a MacArthur Fellow.

Helen Chalakee Burgess is Muscogee (Creek) Indian. She resides in Oklahoma City where she is the Deputy Director of the Oklahoma Indian Affairs Commission. Previously she was communication director for the Muscogee (Creek) Nation and the editor of *The Muscogee Nation News* for ten years. Before that she was the editor of *The Cherokee Advocate* for the Cherokee Nation of Oklahoma. Helen studied journalism at NSU in Tahlequah and has spent much of her time supporting Indian journalism efforts. Believing that today's Indians should not think of culture as having expired with time at a certain date or era, she says, "We are living and creating culture all the time. How we live and what we create and recreate from our Indian minds is an extension of past ideas, habits, customs, attitudes, values, morals, law, and art of our ancestors."From this concept, she says, "Contemporary cultural versions have emerged that highly influence our lives and especially our art forms. We have to believe we are a "revised edition of tradition."Through conflict and accommodation, we have created a cultural hybridism. The reflection of our culture is evident in the everyday life of both rural and urban Indian people. Indian people are living proof that culture is flexible, resilient, and ever changing.

Authors' Biographies

Susan Avery is a writer and editor who has been involved for many years with producing reference books for young people and adults. Her interest in American Indians extends back to college, when she majored in anthropology. She currently lives in western Massachusetts, where she shares a garden with a brooding woodchuck named Joe.

Linda Skinner has twenty years of experience as a teacher, curriculum specialist, teacher trainer, writer, and administrator. She has published a number of curriculum guides and articles, and has presented symposiums in connection with, among others, The Smithsonian Institution, The National Indian Education Association, and the Native American Languages Issues Institute. She was selected Oklahoma Indian Educator of the Year by the Oklahoma Council for Indian Education (1990) and Woman of the Year by the Oklahoma Federation of Indian Women (1990). Ms. Skinner has focused her career on the task of training teachers and developing school curricula that reflect the diversity of Indian and non-Indian cultures. She believes that "early childhood education is the key to our collective future. . . . The thematic, interdisciplinary curriculum, coupled with parent and community involvement can and should reflect the uniqueness of each individual child."